With the help of Hashem

Dedicated In loving Memory of
Tzvi Meir Ben Shlomo Dov Steinmetz
"Tzvi Yair"
By יבלחט״א his wife Devora and his Children

In Gratitude to Hashem
Who has blessed us by helping my father,
Isaac Behar, through his recent illness.
The Behar/Robinson family thank all who have prayed and
supported our family.
May Hashem bless you with all you need.

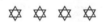

Dedicated by Yaakov Aryeh Leib Halevi
& Nechama Dena Weisman
In Honor of Our Parents
Sherman Israel / Shabsai Yisroel Ben Nissen Halevi Weisman
&
Sylvia Weisman - Altah Sarah bas Hershel

TABLE OF CONTENTS

NEXT SECTION: WORKBOOK REVIEW QUESTIONS

INTRODUCTION

With the help of ה':

Dear Students, Teachers and all who will be using this Pesach Guide!

Greetings and Blessings!

This Updated Edition Pesach Guide contains over eighty five (85) pages of laws, customs and thoughts of our exciting, liberating Yom Tov, Pesach.

Join us as we Journey from the Month of Nissan all the way through Sefirat Ha'omer.

The information in this Pesach Guide is geared to students ages 8 to 108 - grade 3 and up.

100's of Schools and Organizations are learning and teaching with this complete, illustrated textbook and workbook laden with easy-to-read charts and graphs.

This UPDATED EDITION includes the following EXCITING NEW features:

"ROAD TRIP FOR SPIRITUAL FREEDOM"
Truly inspirational MESSAGES FROM PESACH AND THE SIMANEI HASEDER

LYRICS TO PESACH SONGS ~ NEW SEFIRAH CHART ~ AND MORE!

This books is being used by teachers of all influences, grades and ages as a study guide and resource.

Many Jewish Homes are also benefiting from this handy "How To" guide for the content-packed Yom Tov of Pesach!

The laws and customs are geared to the observant and "Hebrew-reading" crowd, as you can see browsing through the pages.

Since there are so many different customs and communities, in this Pesach Guide we try to keep to the "most generic" known customs, as discussed in the "Kitzur Shulchan Aruch" and other "classic" Sefarim.

Included in the back are 280 review questions and charts on the material.

THIS GUIDE'S UNIQUENESS LIES IN THE MANY charts and drawings

THAT HELP CLARIFY THE MATERIAL AND PRESENT IT IN A FUN, EFFECTIVE MANNER.

Please share your corrections, thoughts and suggestions about this book at:

ToolsForTorah@Gmail.com or you can call me at (203) 887 6044.

Please also visit our website: www.ToolsForTorah.com for more fun Tools for Torah!

Thank you!

- Rabbi CB Alevsky

THANK YOU!

This booklet evolved over many years from teaching Halacha to the Elementary grades. The main sources I remember from which I culled most of the material, are: The "Sefer Hatoda'ah" (The Book of our Heritage) by Eliyahu Ki Tov, "Chagainu" by Rabbi E. Wenger, the "Kitzur Shulchan Aruch", the "Shulchan Aruch HaRav", and a variety of Haggadot. I thank the authors of all the above for their contribution.

I would like to thank some of the many people who have helped me with this Pesach Guide. Thank you to...

Rabbi Yosef Hartmann for so carefully and painstakingly reviewing and editing this booklet. You are make yourself available, sharing your broad and deep knowledge with me on this and many other projects.

The Karp Brothers of N.Y. for your constant inspiration and input, and Gershon Eichorn for your guidance in helping me start off many of my projects.

Rabbi G. Steinmetz of Detroit MI. for reviewing the Halachic issues.

Illustrator Tzivi (Dubrowsky) Stolik, for the many patient hours you put into this book, drawing and redrawing as per my many requests.

Rabbi Yossi Hodakov, Chaviva Katz, and Rivka Epstien for combing through the first edition, suggesting, commenting and fixing on almost every page!

Rabbi Y. Goldstein for all the Yiddish translations.

Rabbi Tzvi Freeman/Chabad.org – source of the (revised) Journey to Personal Freedom lessons.

וּמִתַּלְמִידַי יוֹתֵר מִכּוּלָם... Most of all to my students, from Crown Hts. to Long Island, to New Haven and currently of Akiba Academy of Dallas, TX, who have a great share (and lots of fun!) in editing as we learn!

I know there are more – Please forgive me if you helped and I did not mention you.

Last but not least, my wife Sarah and our daughters, Chanah Mushka, Shayna R. and Yehudis Bracha. Thank you for bearing with the countless hours and sleepless nights spent at the computer. Thank you Sarah for introducing and editing the beautiful Freedom lessons and questions for this edition! Thank you for your professional touch regarding the content, style and layout of all my work.(By the way – Sarah is a true world-class graphic designer. Email her if you can use her services: SarahAlevsky@Gmail.com.)

Thank you all. May 'ה give you all health joy and abundance of everything else you want and need לְטוֹבָה.

I really do look forward to your corrections comments and suggestions, to help make the next printing even better! Please share your thoughts! Email them to: ToolsForTorah@Gmail.com

Or call (203) 887 6044. Please also visit our website: www.ToolsForTorah.com.

These books are SPONSORED by people who
DEDICATE a printing to SOMEONE SPECIAL,
or in the MEMORY of a LOVED ONE

Please contact me for future dedication opportunities
for any of our TOOLS FOR TORAH materials.

In the זְכוּת of studying these הֲלָכוֹת, may we merit the true, final and eternal יְצִיאַת מִצְרַיִם - our redemption from our גָלוּת even before נִיסָן - in this joyous month of אֲדָר, and we should say for once and for all times: לַיְּהוּדִים הָיְתָה אוֹרָה וְשִׂמְחָה וְשָׂשֹׂן וִיקָר with the coming of מָשִׁיחַ צִדְקֵנוּ NOW!

Rabbi Chaim B. Alevsky,
Adar 5767 - February 2007
Plano, TX

PESACH: OUR JOURNEY TO FREEDOM!

The story of Pesach, again? I've been learning this stuff since Preschool and I can tell it to you in my sleep! Here goes...

On Pesach we celebrate our freedom from Egyptian slavery by Hashem through His loyal servant, Moshe Rabeinu. Scary plagues rained down on Egypt, and stormy meetings took place between Pharaoh and Moshe. The Jewish People ate a festive meal ending with the Korban Pesach as the Angel of Death passed over their homes, with the doorposts marked with blood.

It's a great story, full of exciting twists and turns, and it ends with the Jewish people marching across the Red Sea and through the desert sands to receive the Holy Torah from Hashem.

Did I get it right? Is there more? Can we close this book now?

That was pretty good – but there is a LOT more. Tell me...

Why do we need a 15-step, complicated Seder to remember the story of Pesach? It says in the Torah it's a Mitzvah to tell the story of Yitziat Mitzrayim. Why can't we just gather and listen to the story, like when we hear the Megillah being read on Purim?

The answer lies in the fact that Pesach is not "just another" holiday. It is a very special holiday.

It was during the course of the Exodus from Egypt that something very holy, very special happened: The Jewish people were transformed from slaves into a nation whose king would be none other than Hashem himself.

During the course of Yitziyat Mitzrayim, we experienced and saw fantastic miracles, the likes of which were never seen before or afterwards.

Our Sages tell us: בְּכָל דּוֹר וָדוֹר, חַיָּיב אָדָם לִרְאוֹת אֶת עַצְמוֹ, כְּאִלּוּ הוּא יָצָא מִמִּצְרָיִם. "In every generation, a person must see himself as if he personally left Egypt."

Our rabbis explain: Even today, we must <u>constantly</u> see ourselves as if we are leaving our own "slavery".

Let's look at our lives today. Are we slaves, doing back-breaking labor? Nope. Are we allowed to study Torah and do Mitzvot in freedom? Yup.

So how can I see myself being freed, when I am already free?

The answer lies in our knowing what freedom really means.

To be slaves isn't just being chained and made to work for others. To be free isn't just being given the chance to do whatever we want, whenever we want.

Every Jewish person possesses a Neshama, a G-dly soul, a part of Hashem himself. This spark of Hashem is infinite, as is Hashem Himself. It is as free as free can be.

Our holy Neshama wants us to learn Torah and do Mitzvot. It wants us to be respectful, kind and helpful, and help make this world a better place.

PESACH: OUR JOURNEY TO FREEDOM!

But our Neshama is challenged by a dark force inside of us: The Yetzer Harah, a sneaky little influence that can convince us to think just about ourselves and no one else. He constantly gets us to think, speak and do things that are not good. And unfortunately, the Yetzer Harah, our personal mini-Pharaoh, is very good at his job!

When we do the wrong thing - even if it is fun or makes us feel good, for a short time - *we become a slave to the Yetzer Harah*. Because in his sneaky way, the Yetzer Harah has gotten us under his spell and made us do what HE wants. Is that freedom, doing the will of the Yetzer Harah? I don't think so....

But don't worry... because the powerful Neshama is coming to the rescue! Your holy Neshama doesn't want the Yetzer Harah/Mini Pharaoh to win. Your soul wants you to be free to do Torah and Mitzvot. When we listen to our Neshama, we are freeing ourselves from our little Pharaoh who wants us to remain "slaves" to him.

Our Rabbis tell us that Mitzrayim (Egypt) is not just a place, but it is also a state of mind. The word מצרים has the root מצר, meaning boundaries and limitations and צר, which means narrow and sorrow. Each of us has our own little מצרים from which we need to escape! We need to break free of what holds us back from doing the right thing.

Now, let's get back to the Seder. How does this long ceremony with its three Matzot and four cups of wine and long Hagadah reading help us experience our personal freedom?

Because every step of the Seder is designed to help move us out of our personal slavery to experience the true freedom we really want, deep down inside our soul.

As we journey through the month of Nissan, preparing for Pesach, as we bake the Matzah and clean our homes... onto the 15 steps of the Seder, we will see all along how each of the steps are also part of our personal יְצִיאַת מִצְרַיִם – our own journey to free ourselves, from ourselves. This journey begins with cleaning and ridding our homes from Chometz and continues to the end of the Seder. This cute little car you see on the left will be a sign that you've reached a Stop n' Study area on our Personal Journey to Freedom. So pull over to the side, turn off the engine and listen to Pesach's message that will help Change Your Life – For Good!

So while you use this book to learn about Pesach, the Seder and all its laws and customs, you will also learn how you can become truly free. And as we end the Seder with the words, *L'shanah Haba'ah Biryushalyim*, may we experience the ultimate freedom for all of us, for all time, with the immediate coming of Moshiach.

Hit the road!

THE MONTH OF NISSAN - חוֹדֶשׁ נִיסָן

This month shall be the HEAD OF THE MONTHS for you	הַחֹדֶשׁ הַזֶּה לָכֶם רֹאשׁ חֳדָשִׁים
It shall be the FIRST MONTH of the year for you (Shemot 12:2)	רִאשׁוֹן הוּא לָכֶם לְחָדְשֵׁי הַשָּׁנָה (שְׁמוֹת יב:ב)
...Seven days you shall eat Matzot as I commanded you at the appointed time in the MONTH OF AVIV (Ripening of grains / Spring)... (Shemot 23:15)	...שִׁבְעַת יָמִים תֹּאכַל מַצּוֹת כַּאֲשֶׁר צִוִּיתִךָ, לְמוֹעֵד חֹדֶשׁ הָאָבִיב... (שְׁמוֹת כג:טו)

נִיסָן is a special month for the Jewish People. נִיסָן arrives in the spring season and this is the יוֹם טוֹב in which we thank Hashem and celebrate the miraculous freedom from our slavery in מִצְרַיִם. This is when we actually became an independent Nation, Hashem's Holy, Chosen Nation.

The very name נִיסָן hints to "נִיסֵי נִיסִים" - miraculous miracles!

In the תּוֹרָה, the month[1] of נִיסָן has two names:

	NAME	TRANSLATION	EXPLANATION
	הַחֹדֶשׁ הָרִאשׁוֹן	The first month	This is the first month in which we were free from our slavery, and became our own Nation. This is why we begin counting our months from נִיסָן.
	חוֹדֶשׁ הָאָבִיב	The month of Spring (Ripening of the Grain)	This month is the Spring season, when the first grain's are ripe.

---

[1] The names of the Jewish months, as we know them - נִיסָן, אַיָּיר, סִיוָן etc. are not mentioned in the תּוֹרָה. They were brought to us by the Jews of בָּבֶל - Babylon, when they returned from their exile.

In our תְּפִלָה:

What	WHEN	WHY
We say a little paragraph called the "נָשִׂיא" and a יְהִי רָצוֹן that follows.	After שַׁחֲרִית, daily, from רֹאשׁ חוֹדֶשׁ נִיסָן until י"ג נִיסָן.	The מִשְׁכָּן was completed and set up in the מִדְבָּר, on רֹאשׁ חוֹדֶשׁ נִיסָן. For the next twelve days, the נְשִׂיאִים (leaders) of all the שְׁבָטִים offered presents to ה' to consecrate (make holy / dedicate) the מִשְׁכָּן. The "נָשִׂיא" we read, is the description of the daily offerings which the נְשִׂיאִים of each שֵׁבֶט brought.

Each of the 12 נְשִׂיאִים offered the exact same presents to Hashem.

These are the presents the נְשִׂיאִים offered:

#	What	Last Known Picture	Weighing	Filled with	For
1	Silver Bowl		130 Shekels	Fine Flour mixed with Olive Oil	A Meal Offering
1	Silver Sprinkling Basin		70 Shekels	Fine Flour mixed with Olive Oil	Meal Offering
1	Spoon		10 Gold Shekels	Incense	
1	Young Bull, Ram, & Lamb				Burnt Offering
1	Young He Goat				Sin Offering
2	Oxen				Peace Offering
5	Rams, He Goats & Lambs		Broke the scale!		Peace Offering

When the תּוֹרָה tells us about the presents, the תּוֹרָה repeats all the details of the offerings 12x... over and over and over and over and over and over and over and over and over and over and over again! (*whew!*) Only the names are changed for each time.

Why didn't the תּוֹרָה just list all the presents once, and mention that each נָשִׂיא brought the same thing?

One reason is because each of the leaders had different כַּוָּונוֹת (intentions / focus / thoughts) when they brought their offerings. The Midrash describes "what they were thinking" when they brought their presents, and each of them had different כַּוָּונוֹת – they each intended for their presents to represent different ideas.

Two sweet lessons for us: While many people do the same מִצְוֹות, the intentions can be very different.

Also, while we do the same מִצְוֹות every day (like תְּפִילָה, learning and אַהֲבַת יִשְׂרָאֵל etc.), we can and should always do them with more intense כַּוָּונָה.

The "נָשִׂיא" can be found in a חוּמָשׁ in פֶּרֶק ז פִּי נָשֹא, or in a סִידוּר. In some Shuls, the נָשִׂיא is read from the תּוֹרָה. For this reading, men are not called up to the תּוֹרָה and the נָשִׂיא is read without making any בְּרָכָה.

During the entire month of נִיסָן we don't say תַּחֲנוּן.

DOODLE YOURSELF DAVENING:

MONEY FOR WHEAT (MATZOT) - מָעוֹת חִטִּים

If there will be among you a needy (poor man) of your brethren	כִּי יִהְיֶה בְךָ אֶבְיוֹן מֵאַחַד אַחֶיךָ....
DO NOT HARDEN YOUR HEART, OR SHUT YOUR HAND against your needy brother	לֹא תְאַמֵּץ אֶת לְבָבְךָ וְלֹא תִקְפֹּץ אֶת יָדְךָ מֵאָחִיךָ הָאֶבְיוֹן
But YOU SHALL SURELY OPEN YOUR HAND TO HIM, and (if he does not want to take it – then...) surely lend him what he needs... (Devarim 15:7-8)	כִּי פָתֹחַ תִּפְתַּח אֶת יָדְךָ לוֹ וְהַעֲבֵט תַּעֲבִיטֶנּוּ דֵּי מַחְסֹרוֹ אֲשֶׁר יֶחְסַר לוֹ (דברים טו:ז-ח)

During חוֹדֶשׁ נִיסָן, it is most important to give צְדָקָה in the form of מָעוֹת חִטִּים - money for wheat. This money is distributed to the poor, to help supply them with מַצּוֹת and other necessities for פֶּסַח.

On פֶּסַח we are meant to conduct ourselves in a "royal" manner, like kings. It is much "kinglyer" for us to sit down to our סֵדֶר in our home, knowing that we helped provide our brethren with all that they need for their סֵדֶר!

❈ ❈ ❈ ❈ ❈ ❈ ❈ ❈ ❈ ❈ ❈ ❈ ❈

BUILD YOUR APPETITE!

In order to increase our appetite for the מַצָּה on פֶּסַח, we do not eat מַצָּה on עֶרֶב פֶּסַח.

Some have the custom not to eat מַצָּה from רֹאשׁ חוֹדֶשׁ נִיסָן, and some begin this custom from פּוּרִים - one month before פֶּסַח.

SHABBAT HAGGADOL - שַׁבָּת הַגָּדוֹל

On the 10th of this month every man must take for himself a lamb for each family, a lamb for each household (Shemot 12:3)	בֶּעָשׂר לַחֹדֶשׁ הַזֶּה וְיִקְחוּ לָהֶם אִישׁ שֶׂה לְבֵית אָבֹת שֶׂה לַבָּיִת (שְׁמוֹת יב:ג)
And you shall hold it in safekeeping until the 14th day of this month	וְהָיָה לָכֶם לְמִשְׁמֶרֶת עַד אַרְבָּעָה עָשָׂר יוֹם לַחֹדֶשׁ הַזֶּה
And the whole community of Israel shall slaughter it in the afternoon (Shemot 12:6)	וְשָׁחֲטוּ אֹתוֹ כֹּל קְהַל עֲדַת יִשְׂרָאֵל בֵּין הָעַרְבָּיִם (שְׁמוֹת יב: ו)

The שַׁבָּת before פֶּסַח is called שַׁבָּת הַגָּדוֹל - the "great, big" or "important" שַׁבָּת.

There are a quite a few reasons for this name, some of them are:

1.   Before leaving מִצְרַיִם, the Jewish People took a lamb into their homes, tied it to their beds, and prepared it for the קָרְבָּן פֶּסַח. This happened on the tenth day of נִיסָן which fell that year on שַׁבָּת. When asked by the מִצְרַיִם what they were doing, בְּנֵי יִשְׂרָאֵל answered that they were going to slaughter the lamb as a קָרְבָּן פֶּסַח, like ה׳ told them to. The מִצְרִים were very mad that בְּנֵי יִשְׂרָאֵל were going to "*shecht*" their "god", and tried to hurt בְּנֵי יִשְׂרָאֵל, but failed, for ה׳ caused them pain and suffering when they tried to do harm. Since this great נֵס occurred on this שַׁבָּת, it is called שַׁבָּת הַגָּדוֹל.

2.   During that time, the בְּכוֹרֵי מִצְרַיִם (firstborn) found out that ה׳ was going to kill them in מַכַּת בְּכוֹרוֹת. When they saw their "god" (עֲבוֹדָה זָרָה) tied to the beds, they thought to themselves, "now, surely this we will die, for we have no more protection..." The frightened first born ran to their parents and to פַּרְעֹה begging them to let בְּנֵי יִשְׂרָאֵל leave מִצְרַיִם. The authorities refused to hear of it but the first born were not willing to die so easily... they waged war with the rest of מִצְרַיִם, killing many of their own. This is hinted in the words "לְמַכֵּה מִצְרַיִם בִּבְכוֹרֵיהֶם - He smote (struck/killed) מִצְרַיִם *with* their firstborn" meaning *through* their firstborn.

3.   On this day, the גָדוֹל הָעִיר - the "important" member of the city – usually the רַב - gives a "big, long" speech, reviewing "הֲלָכוֹת גְדוֹלוֹת" - big important laws of פֶּסַח.

4.   On this day, בְּנֵי יִשְׂרָאֵל were commanded their first commandment as a Nation, to offer the קָרְבָּן פֶּסַח. This is comparable to a בַּר or בַּת מִצְוָה, at which time a young child becomes a גָדוֹל or גְדוֹלָה - an adult, and is obligated and responsible to fulfill all the מִצְוֹת.

5.   Ever since בְּנֵי יִשְׂרָאֵל were freed, we "paired up" with the שַׁבָּת. As the *Midrash* relates, that the "שַׁבָּת" complained to 'ה that each day of the week has its "pair", Sunday had Monday etc., but שַׁבָּת, being an odd number, was the only "single" one. 'ה promised that בְּנֵי יִשְׂרָאֵל would "pair up" with שַׁבָּת. Through בְּנֵי יִשְׂרָאֵל keeping the שַׁבָּת holy the שַׁבָּת itself finally paired up became greater and more important.

6.   At the end of the הַפְטָרָה of this week, we read about the time when מָשִׁיחַ will come. The פְּסוּקִים describe a יוֹם הַגָדוֹל וְהַנוֹרָא - a "great and awesome day." (This is similar to the way שַׁבָּת שׁוּבָה and שַׁבָּת חֲזוֹן received their names from their הַפְטָרוֹת).

7.   בְּנֵי יִשְׂרָאֵל crossed over the יַרְדֵן - Jordan river, on their way to אֶרֶץ יִשְׂרָאֵל, on this שַׁבָּת, the 10th day of נִיסָן.

8.   Another amusing reason (which רש"י gives) for this name: On שַׁבָּת הַגָדוֹל, the רַב of the *Shul* says the דְרָשָׁה about the דִינִים of פֶּסַח. He reviews the laws with the קָהָל, and discusses the current issues. Since is takes quite a while to cover all the necessary material... - it seems to the people in *Shul*, that the day is l o n g e r than usual... that is why it's called "שַׁבָּת הַגָדוֹל."

DOODLE YOUR SHUL:

THE TIMING OF SHABBAT HAGGADOL

Q: Why do we celebrate the שַׁבָּת הַגָּדוֹל specifically on שַׁבָּת? The נֵס happened on י' נִיסָן, and usually we celebrate a יוֹם טוֹב or any other special day, by its <u>date</u> in the <u>month</u>, not the <u>day</u> of the <u>week</u>.

A: On this date - י' נִיסָן - 39 years later, מֹשֶׁה's sister מִרְיָם הַנְבִיאָה passed away. The "well of מִרְיָם" also stopped flowing at that time. Therefore, the חֲכָמִים established that the "celebration" for the good things that happened should take place on שַׁבָּת, the day of the week, rather than the day of the month. (When this date falls out on a weekday, some people fast in memory of מִרְיָם הַנְבִיאָה.)

On שַׁבָּת הַגָּדוֹל we say part of the הַגָּדָה:

WHEN	WHAT	WHY
שַׁבָּת הַגָּדוֹל after מִנְחָה	From עֲבָדִים הָיִינוּ, until לְכַפֵּר עַל כָּל עֲוֹנוֹתֵינוּ	1. The beginning of the גְאוּלָה started on this day, so we "talk" about it. 2. To familiarize ourselves with the הַגָּדָה which we will soon be saying at our סֵדֶר.

חַג הַפֶּסַח - PESACH

Keep the festival of Matzot	אֶת חַג הַמַּצּוֹת תִּשְׁמֹר
...at the appointed time of the month of "Aviv"	לְמוֹעֵד חֹדֶשׁ הָאָבִיב...
Because in it (in this time) you went out of Egypt (Shemot 23:15)	כִּי בוֹ יָצָאתָ מִמִּצְרַיִם (שמות כג: טו)
...And I will see the blood and I will PASS OVER you	...וְרָאִיתִי אֶת הַדָּם וּפָסַחְתִּי עֲלֵכֶם
And there won't be a deadly plague amongst you (Shemot 12:13)	וְלֹא יִהְיֶה בָכֶם נֶגֶף לְמַשְׁחִית (שמות יב,יג)

On פֶּסַח we celebrate that ה' freed us from the Egyptian slavery and took us to be His very own holy nation!

We were freed on the 15th day of Nissan in the year 2448 after the creation of the world.

ה' plagued מִצְרַיִם with awesome wonders and miracles, including the 10 מַכּוֹת, and made us into His Holy Nation.

ה' told בְּנֵי יִשְׂרָאֵל to offer a lamb as a קָרְבָּן פֶּסַח and smear some of its blood onto the doorposts and lintel (top of doorpost). Then, when he struck all the firstborn of מִצְרַיִם, with the last מַכָּה - He PASSED OVER the homes with the קָרְבָּן blood on the doorposts. Commemorating this נֵס, the firstborn of each family fasts on עֶרֶב פֶּסַח.

Hashem instructs us to celebrate פֶּסַח every year at this time by eating מַצָּה, not eating חָמֵץ, and by telling the story of יְצִיאַת מִצְרַיִם.

A very interesting note about the blood on the doorposts: The shape of the blood on the door was similar to the letter ה. The lintel (top of the doorpost) and the two sides. This was hinting to ה' who would pass over these doors and guard those who were inside!

(SOME OF THE) מִצְוֹת OF חַג הַפֶּסַח

(These מִצְוֹת will be explained in detail, in the next few pages)

	What	In the תּוֹרָה it says...
1	Not to eat חָמֵץ all seven days of פֶּסַח (Shemot 12:17...)	כִּי כָּל אֹכֵל חָמֵץ וְנִכְרְתָה הַנֶּפֶשׁ הַהִוא מִיִּשְׂרָאֵל מִיּוֹם הָרִאשׁן עַד יוֹם הַשְּׁבִעִי (שמות יב:יז...)
2	Not to <u>have</u> חָמֵץ in our possession all seven days of פֶּסַח	שִׁבְעַת יָמִים שְׂאֹר לֹא יִמָּצֵא בְּבָתֵּיכֶם
3	Not to <u>see</u> חָמֵץ in our possession all seven days of פֶּסַח	...וְלֹא יֵרָאֶה לְךָ חָמֵץ...
4	To <u>eat</u> מַצָּה for seven days[2]	שִׁבְעַת יָמִים תֹּאכַל מַצּוֹת
5	To tell the story of יְצִיאַת מִצְרַיִם on the 1st night of פֶּסַח (Shemot 13:8)	וְהִגַּדְתָּ לְבִנְךָ, בַּיּוֹם הַהוּא לֵאמֹר בַּעֲבוּר זֶה עָשָׂה ה' לִי בְּצֵאתִי מִמִּצְרַיִם (שמות יג:ח)

NAMES OF פֶּסַח

	NAME	MEANING	EXPLANATION
	חַג הַפֶּסַח	The Holiday of Passover	ה' passed over (skipped) the houses of בְּנֵי יִשְׂרָאֵל when all the בְּכוֹרֵי מִצְרַיִם were being killed.
	חַג הַמַּצּוֹת	The Holiday of Matzos	We are commanded to eat מַצּוֹת during the week of פֶּסַח.
	חַג הָאָבִיב	The Holiday of the Spring / Ripening of the Grain	ה' commanded us that פֶּסַח should always be celebrated during the spring season.[3]
	זְמַן חֵירוּתֵנוּ	The time of our Freedom (Redemption)	We were freed from the Egyptian slavery in this month.

---

[2] רמב״ם explains that we are obligated to (we must) eat מַצָּה on the 1st night of פֶּסַח – and from then on, for the rest of Pesach, it is optional – if we want to eat מַצָּה - wonderful, if not, we do not need to.
We MUST be sure about not having חָמֵץ all seven days.

So many names... What's its real name?!

ה' - in the תּוֹרָה - calls this יוֹם טוֹב with one name, and we - בְּנֵי יִשְׂרָאֵל call it with a different name. We each have our own special reasons:

WHO	CALLS IT	WHY
ה'	חַג הַמַּצּוֹת	The קָרְבַּן פֶּסַח was brought only one day, on the day before the first day of פֶּסַח. The מִצְוָה of eating מַצָּה however, is throughout the entire week of פֶּסַח. ה' loves when we do His מִצְווֹת, and therefore calls the יוֹם טוֹב by the "longer" מִצְוָה, the one we fulfill for a greater period of time.
בְּנֵי יִשְׂרָאֵל	פֶּסַח	We are referring to the קָרְבַּן פֶּסַח. While the בֵּית הַמִּקְדָּשׁ was standing, בְּנֵי יִשְׂרָאֵל celebrated פֶּסַח by bringing a קָרְבַּן פֶּסַח. This was a great experience in which everyone participated. Unfortunately, today, until the בֵּית הַמִּקְדָּשׁ will be rebuilt, we cannot offer our קָרְבַּן פֶּסַח. Therefore, we call the יוֹם טוֹב with the name פֶּסַח, to remember the קָרְבַּן פֶּסַח that we really want to offer to ה', but can't. We hope that when ה' hears us talk about the "פֶּסַח", He will bring מָשִׁיחַ and build the בֵּית הַמִּקְדָּשׁ, so that even this year, we will be able offer the קָרְבַּן properly!

DOODLE YOUR JEWISH NAME:

Rabbi לֵוִי יִצְחָק of *Berditchov* a beautiful explanation on these יום טוב names:

We, בְּנֵי יִשְׂרָאֵל love 'ה so much, we always want to talk about the wonderful things He has done, and does for us, and we love to praise Him for them.

'ה loves בְּנֵי יִשְׂרָאֵל so much, He always wants to remember the good things we did and do for Him, and 'ה loves praising us for them.

That is why:

We call it פֶּסַח - because 'ה had "passed over" and skipped the Jewish homes, when He was punishing the people of מִצְרַיִם. We thank 'ה for this, by calling the יום טוב by the name which "tells" us about it - פֶּסַח!

'ה calls it חַג הַמַצוֹת. This is to remember and praise us - בְּנֵי יִשְׂרָאֵל, for leaving מִצְרַיִם to go into the desert as soon as He told us to, without letting our dough rise into bread. We didn't prepare any other food for the journey in the desert, even though we knew we would be there for a while... and there was no food there for us. We trusted that 'ה would take good care of us!

This is one of the reasons why מַצָה is called the Bread Of Faith. It shows our אֱמוּנָה - faith in 'ה, that we listen to Him immediately, without hesitation, and trust in Him that He will take care of us.

This way, 'ה calls this יום טוב by the name that praises us – his very own, precious בְּנֵי יִשְׂרָאֵל!

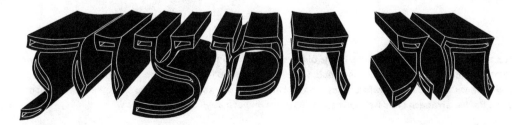

THE פֶּסַח CALENDAR

And the first day shall be a sacred (holy) Holiday and the seventh shall be a sacred Holiday for you.	וּבַיּוֹם הָרִאשׁוֹן מִקְרָא קֹדֶשׁ וּבַיּוֹם הַשְּׁבִיעִי מִקְרָא קֹדֶשׁ יִהְיֶה לָכֶם
No work shall be done in them (those days)	כָּל-מְלָאכָה לֹא יֵעָשֶׂה בָהֶם
The only work that you may do, is that which is needed so that everyone will be able to eat. (Shemot 12:16)	אַךְ אֲשֶׁר יֵאָכֵל לְכָל נֶפֶשׁ הוּא לְבַדּוֹ יֵעָשֶׂה לָכֶם (שמות יב:טז)

As you see in the above פְּסוּקִים, the תּוֹרָה calls the יוֹם הָרִאשׁוֹן – the first day, and the יוֹם הַשְּׁבִיעִי – the seventh day – מִקְרָאֵי קוֹדֶשׁ – holy days of יוֹם טוֹב.

Our חֲכָמִים added another day to each of these days, and now we celebrate two days in place of the first day of פֶּסַח and two days in place of the seventh day of פֶּסַח.

The 2nd day of יוֹם טוֹב is called: יוֹם טוֹב שֵׁנִי שֶׁל גָּלוּיוֹת[4] - the 2nd day of יוֹם טוֹב - that is celebrated in the exiles, meaning outside of אֶרֶץ יִשְׂרָאֵל.

In חוּץ לָאָרֶץ – outside of Israel - all יָמִים טוֹבִים have the יוֹם טוֹב שֵׁנִי – the "extra" day[5]. We have two סְדָרִים on פֶּסַח, two days of שָׁבוּעוֹת (let's not forget the cheesecake!) and two days of יוֹם טוֹב in the beginning of סֻכּוֹת.

רֹאשׁ הַשָּׁנָה is the only יוֹם טוֹב that is celebrated for two days even in אֶרֶץ יִשְׂרָאֵל.

The יוֹם טוֹב of פֶּסַח begins טו נִיסָן and continues for 8 days until כב נִיסָן.

The first 2 days are מִקְרָאֵי קוֹדֶשׁ, or יוֹם טוֹב - meaning that these days are אָסוּר בִּמְלָאכָה - we are not allowed to do any מְלָאכָה - "work" that is forbidden on שַׁבָּת - we are however, allowed to do מְלָאכוֹת that are necessary for food preparation.

---

[4] Our חֲכָמִים established this 2nd day of יוֹם טוֹב because in the olden days רֹאשׁ חוֹדֶשׁ was established when the new moon was spotted, and the בֵּית דִּין in יְרוּשָׁלַיִם sent messages out to all the people to tell them when רֹאשׁ חוֹדֶשׁ is. The people who lived far from יְרוּשָׁלַיִם were not sure which day רֹאשׁ חוֹדֶשׁ would be. Therefore, they did not know what day to celebrate the יוֹם טוֹב in that month – i.e. Sunday or Monday... The Rabbis arranged that we celebrate the יוֹם טוֹב on both days on which there was a doubt, - i.e. Sunday and Monday.

[5] Besides יוֹם כִּפּוּר. We don't celebrate 2 days of יוֹם כִּפּוּר - because it is too hard to fast 2 days straight!

We celebrate and experience the סֵדֶר the first two days – which are יוֹם טוֹב - the 15th and 16th of נִיסָן. The next 4 days are חוֹל הַמּוֹעֵד - "the weekdays of the יוֹם טוֹב", on which we may do most kinds of מְלָאכוֹת.[6] The last 2 days are יוֹם טוֹב again - days of מִקְרָאֵי קוֹדֶשׁ which are also אָסוּר בִּמְלָאכָה. We call the last 2 days: שְׁבִיעִי שֶׁל פֶּסַח and אַחֲרוֹן שֶׁל פֶּסַח.

This is the פֶּסַח calendar:

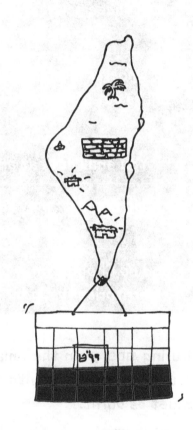

Date	Day		We...
טו נִיסָן	1	1st day of יוֹם טוֹב	Celebrate 1st סֵדֶר
טז נִיסָן	2	2nd day of יוֹם טוֹב	Celebrate 2nd סֵדֶר
יז נִיסָן	3	1st day of חוֹל הַמּוֹעֵד	Family time!
חי נִיסָן	4	2nd day of חוֹל הַמּוֹעֵד	Family time!
יט נִיסָן	5	3rd day of חוֹל הַמּוֹעֵד	Family time!
כ נִיסָן	6	4th day of חוֹל הַמּוֹעֵד	Family time!
כא נִיסָן	7	שְׁבִיעִי שֶׁל פֶּסַח	יוֹם טוֹב
כב נִיסָן	8	אַחֲרוֹן שֶׁל פֶּסַח	יוֹם טוֹב

All this occurs in חוּץ לָאָרֶץ - (outside of אֶרֶץ יִשְׂרָאֵל).

In אֶרֶץ יִשְׂרָאֵל however, the schedule is a little different.

- In אֶרֶץ יִשְׂרָאֵל they celebrate only *one* day of יוֹם טוֹב in the beginning, instead of two days. They have only <u>one</u> סֵדֶר.

- In אֶרֶץ יִשְׂרָאֵל they celebrate 5 days of חוֹל הַמּוֹעֵד, and celebrate שְׁבִיעִי שֶׁל פֶּסַח and אַחֲרוֹן שֶׁל פֶּסַח on the *same* day, - the 7th day.

- The 8th day is not יוֹם טוֹב in אֶרֶץ יִשְׂרָאֵל.

---

[6] And go to the zoo...

CHAMETZ – חָמֵץ

For seven days you should eat Matzos	שִׁבְעַת יָמִים מַצּוֹת תֹּאכֵלוּ
On the first day you should remove Chometz from your homes (Shemot 12:15)	...בַּיּוֹם הָרִאשׁוֹן תַּשְׁבִּיתוּ שְּׂאֹר מִבָּתֵּיכֶם (שמות יב:ט"ו)
During these seven days Chometz may not be found in your homes	שִׁבְעַת יָמִים שְׂאֹר לֹא יִמָּצֵא בְּבָתֵּיכֶם
For whoever will each Chometz, that soul will be cut off from (the community of) Israel	כִּי כָּל אֹכֵל חָמֵץ וְנִכְרְתָה הַנֶּפֶשׁ הַהוּא מִיִּשְׂרָאֵל... (שמות יב:יט...)
You shall not eat any Chometz...	כָּל מַחְמֶצֶת לֹא תֹאכֵלוּ
No Chometz may be seen in your possession...	...וְלֹא יֵרָאֶה לְךָ חָמֵץ...
And no Chometz may be seen in all your territories (boundaries) (Shemot: 13:7)	וְלֹא-יֵרָאֶה לְךָ שְׂאֹר בְּכָל-גְּבֻלֶךָ (שמות יג:ז)

During פֶּסַח, even the smallest, tiniest amount of חָמֵץ is forbidden. If the smallest crumb of חָמֵץ falls into the largest amount of "non-חָמֵץ", it is *all* forbidden, and must be burnt.

What is חָמֵץ?

If you take any one of the five grains: wheat, barley, spelt, oats or rye – mix it with water and let it rest for 18 minutes or more – this is חָמֵץ.

On פֶּסַח we are forbidden to own חָמֵץ.

Draw some wheat:

The Spiritual חָמֵץ

There is also a spiritual חָמֵץ that we need to be careful to remove.

חָמֵץ is compared to the יֵצֶר הָרַע, while מַצָּה, is compared to the יֵצֶר טוֹב.

We see this in many ways:

חָמֵץ and מַצָה can have the same ingredients and still "act" very different.

חָמֵץ usually tastes better than מַצָה.

חָמֵץ usually looks better than מַצָה.

חָמֵץ is "puffy" and blown up, while מַצָה is flat.

Similarly, the יֵצֶר הָרַע tries to make wrong things look better and nicer than they really are.

חָמֵץ and מַצָה also symbolize the way a person acts: מַצָּה is flat and humble, and חָמֵץ, even though it has the exact same ingredients is more "puffed up", haughty and boastful.

So too, חָמֵץ acts like a "show off." Even though it is made of the same stuff מַצָה is, it still acts like it is better.

One of the differences between a humble and haughty person, is that a humble person tries to always find the good things about other people, and compliments them about the good things they find.

The haughty person does the opposite. He or she will look for a fault, or "not so good" thing about another and point it out. The haughty person thinks that s/he becomes "bigger" by putting someone else down.

The humble person knows that the opposite is true. The better you are, the more you compliment others!

DOODLE A MATZAH:

The words חָמֵץ and מַצָּה, have similar letters. Both words have a מ and a צ. The only difference is the ח and the ה. Even these two letters are very similar, only a very small line sets apart the ח from the ה.

ח	צ	מ
ה	צ	מ

We can see that the ח of the חָמֵץ has no opening at the top of the letter, while the ה of the מַצָּה does. This tells us that when one that acts in a "way of חָמֵץ" he can get stuck and have a hard time "getting out", (the only way is down...) while the "מַצָּה person" has an "easy escape", and can get closer to 'ה easier.

This tiny difference in the letters also shows us that מַצָּה can turn into חָמֵץ very easily.

Another beautiful lesson:
In order for the dough of מַצָּה to become חָמֵץ, you don't even have to *do* anything – just *let it res.* It will automatically turn into חָמֵץ. This shows us, that we must always "work" with ourselves to be better than we already are. If we just "rest" and "relax" in our personal spiritual growth – we might already be turning into חָמֵץ...

◆ We search for חָמֵץ on the night after the 13th of נִיסָן. This also represents the 13th year, the *Bar Mitzvah*. It is at this time that he must search for and totally remove any possible "leftover" חָמֵץ that he might still have.

CLEANING FOR PESACH!!!

AS THE DUST SETTLES FROM THE PURIM NOSH AND EXCITEMENT...
MOMMY GETS INTO A CONTAGIOUS PESACH CLEANING MODE...
AS WE ALL GET INFECTED... THE CLEANING FRENZY BEGINS!

We spend the few weeks between Purim and Pesach preparing our homes for Pesach.

To ensure our goal - to remove all the Chametz from our homes – we:

Sweep and wash floors, vacuum carpets, scrub tables and chairs, check our drawers and cabinets, Check our clothes pockets and wipe our toys and books clean.

Since it is common to find books on the same tables on which we eat Chametz, we need to wipe the book backs clean from any trace of crumb that may have been gotten stuck. Some people actually flip through the pages of every book in their homes – face down – to allow for any possible crumbs to fall out.

Here are some effective strategies to ensure our victory in our War Against Chametz / Pesach Cleaning Experience:

1. Divide and Conquer:

    a. Split up the jobs and rooms of the house amongst the family members, each child is responsible for a specific room and job.

2. Positioning:

    a. It had been reported that the best way to succeed is to begin from the rooms farthest away and work towards the Kitchen – the main source of the enemy...

    b. As a room is inspected and verified clean – it is labeled: Kosher For Pesach! And no further Chametz may be brought into the room!

3. Final Battle: the Kitchen!

    The Kitchen is the final battleground... as we need to eat regularly until Pesach starts, our kitchen in the last to get cleaned.

    Some things that are used for Chametz year round can be "Kashered" for Pesach use.

The way to Kasher something is to boil or burn it, bringing it to a boiling point or heat level – as hot as it has ever been, while it was in contact with Chametz.

There are many different levels of Kashering things.

    i. Stoves, ovens and grills need to be Kashered with FIRE.

    ii. Pots, pans, silverware, sinks and countertops can often be Kashered with BOILING WATER.

The Kashering Mission is a dangerous one. It must be done by qualified adults with instructions from a qualified Rabbis. Don't try to Kasher at home, alone!

Within the kitchen itself, there are many other areas to tackle the Chametz, Some of them are:

    iii. Food:

        1. All foods that are not Kosher for Pesach must be removed from our home or quarantined for the future Sale to our non Jewish Ally.

    iv. Dishes:

        1. Most Kosher homes today use a separate set of dishes and silverware for Pesach. It is VERY difficult, and sometimes impossible – to *Kasher* some utensils to be fit for Pesach use, after they've been used in Chametz.

    v. Counters:

        1. Countertops must be Kashered for Pesach use. Many homes *Kasher* & Cover their countertops for extra protection.

    vi. Sinks:

        1. Sinks must be Kashered for Pesach use. Many homes *Kasher* & Cover their sinks for extra protection.

    vii. Stove:

        1. Sinks must be Kashered for Pesach use. If your stove has a "Self Cleaning" feature – running it 2x is the easiest way to Kasher it.

        2. Grills must be Kashered for Pesach use. Grills need to be torched by fire until they are sizzling red hot.

    viii. Fridge:

        1. Fridges and freezers need to be thoroughly cleaned for Pesach use. Many homes cover the shelves of the fridge for extra protection.

THE SEARCH FOR *CHOMETZ* – בְּדִיקַת חָמֵץ

There is no specific מִצְוָה in the תּוֹרָה to "search" for חָמֵץ. The מִצְוָה is לְהַשְׁבִּית – to eliminate (get rid of) the חָמֵץ. We eliminate our חָמֵץ by burning it; this is called בִּיעוּר חָמֵץ. Now, in order to burn it – we must first find it! Therefore, the בְּדִיקָה is the *beginning* of the מִצְוָה of the בִּיעוּר.

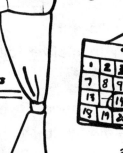

On the night *of* עֶרֶב פֶּסַח, the *night* of the 14th of נִיסָן,[7] we check and search our homes and property for חָמֵץ.

We wait until after the stars come out, because at this time, most people are anyway in their homes.

Before the בְּדִיקָה, our house is already cleaned and prepared for פֶּסַח.

We check all our books that may have been used during the year for crumbs that might have fallen in between the pages. We must also check all our pockets for any leftover crumbs or candy that may be חָמֵץ.

Before the בְּדִיקָה, we prepare:

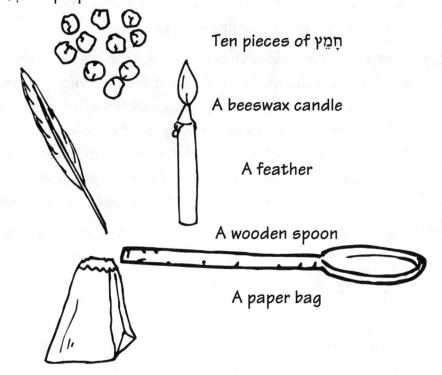

Ten pieces of חָמֵץ

A beeswax candle

A feather

A wooden spoon

A paper bag

---

[7] In the Jewish calendar, the day begins with the previous night.

During the בְּדִיקָה, we will search for leftover חָמֵץ in our home, and also "find" some "planted" pieces of חָמֵץ. This is how it works:

Before the בְּדִיקָה, we prepare ten pieces of חָמֵץ. The חָמֵץ should be a food that does not have lots of crumbs, or does not break apart too easily. Matzah or a hard cracker sounds like a good idea. We wrap the ten pieces in paper, tissue or plastic wrap. We wrap them well, to make sure the crumbs won't fall out. (Some people wrap the חָמֵץ in silver foil – but it is not recommended, because foil doesn't burn.)

We hide these ten pieces of חָמֵץ all around the house. It is <u>very important</u> to note (on paper!) where the חָמֵץ was hidden in the house. It is easy to forget where exactly you hid your חָמֵץ, and not finding it can cause an unnecessary panic!

A spiritual reason for putting out the חָמֵץ is to teach us that even if we clean up our act very well, if we try very hard, we can always find some more to clean up! This is mainly concerning the "spiritual חָמֵץ", the "not so good" things we do, say, or even think. Even if someone works very hard at removing his or her חָמֵץ, and thinks "Now I'm all pure, clean of חָמֵץ... and כָּשֵׁר לְפֶסַח..." He can still find a little more if he honestly examines himself.

For the בְּדִיקָה, we also need a candle with which to search all the nooks, crannies and corners of our home. This candle must be a single wick candle – so we shouldn't be so worried about anything catching fire. It should be made of beeswax – because this type of candle doesn't drip as much as others, which makes it more comfortable to use. A regular candle can be used if you don't have a beeswax one, but it must have only one wick. A *Havdalah* candle may *not* be used.

We use a feather to "sweep" the חָמֵץ we find into a large wooden spoon. The חָמֵץ goes from the spoon into a paper bag.

All these things will be burned the next morning, together with the rest of the חָמֵץ.

Before we start the search, the "head of the household" makes the בְּרָכָה:

"בָּא"י אֱמָ"הָ אֲקַבְּ"ן עַל בִּיעוּר חָמֵץ." Those who hear the בְּרָכָה answer "אָמֵן."

This בְּרָכָה is for the "burning" of the חָמֵץ. There is no separate בְּרָכָה for the "searching" of the חָמֵץ. Some say, this is because there is no מִצְוָה to "search." The מִצְוָה is to *nullify or burn* the חָמֵץ, and the בְּדִיקָה is the *beginning* of the בִּיעוּר.

This בְּרָכָה includes all those who will be searching for the חָמֵץ. We should not talk until after the complete בְּדִיקָה, which ends *after* we say the "כָּל חֲמִירָא", the special declaration that we say to nullify all the חָמֵץ we didn't find during our בְּדִיקָה.

If one has more than one place to do the בְּדִיקָה, like another home, office or other places, he should make one בְּרָכָה for all the places. He could even send "messengers" to search for him in the other places.

After we search, we put away whatever חָמֵץ we found, in a safe place, out of reach of young children or animals that might move the חָמֵץ from one place to another. In that same place, we keep the food that we are going to eat the next morning, which is also חָמֵץ.

If the בְּדִיקָה was not done on this night, then it should be done anytime until and during פֶּסַח. If it is during פֶּסַח, we still make the בְּרָכָה. After פֶּסַח the בְּדִיקָה is done without a בְּרָכָה.

חָמֵץ that remained in the possession of a Jew during פֶּסַח, is called "חָמֵץ שֶׁעָבַר עָלָיו הַפֶּסַח" – Chometz that "survived" (lived through) the Pesach. We are forbidden to have any benefit or "pleasure" from חָמֵץ that was in our possession during פֶּסַח. This חָמֵץ must be burnt even after פֶּסַח. We do not make a בְּרָכָה for this burning.

If you leave your house within *one month* before פֶּסַח, even if you do not plan to return before פֶּסַח, you should clean your house, and search for חָמֵץ the night before you leave, without a בְּרָכָה. If you leave before that, and you do not plan to return before פֶּסַח - it is not necessary.

When עֶרֶב פֶּסַח falls out on a שַׁבָּת, then, since the בְּדִיקָה night is Friday night, and we *cannot* search for the חָמֵץ then, we do it on the previous night - Thursday night.

BURNING THE CHOMETZ – בִּיעוּר חָמֵץ

On the first day you should remove Chometz from your homes (Shemot 12:15)	...בַּיוֹם הָרִאשׁוֹן תַּשְׁבִּיתוּ שְּׂאֹר מִבָּתֵּיכֶם (שמות יב: טו)
During these seven days Chometz may not be found in your homes (Shemot 12:19)	שִׁבְעַת יָמִים שְׂאֹר לֹא יִמָּצֵא בְּבָתֵּיכֶם (שמות יב:יט)
No Chometz may be seen in your possession...	...וְלֹא יֵרָאֶה לְךָ חָמֵץ...
And no Chometz may be seen in all your territories (boundaries) (Shemot: 13:7)	וְלֹא יֵרָאֶה לְךָ שְׂאֹר בְּכָל-גְּבֻלֶךָ (שמות יג:ז)
You should not slaughter the קָרְבַּן פֶּסַח with חָמֵץ (still in your possession) (Shemot: 34:25)	לֹא תִשְׁחַט עַל חָמֵץ דַּם זִבְחִי (שמות לד:כה)
You should not eat חָמֵץ with it. (Shemot 16:3)	לֹא תֹאכַל עָלָיו חָמֵץ (שמות טז:ג)

The תּוֹרָה says לֹא יִמָּצֵא בְּבָתֵּיכֶם and וְלֹא יֵרָאֶה לְךָ חָמֵץ - which means that חָמֵץ may not be *seen*, and may not be *found* in our possession during פֶּסַח.

We are commanded to *remove* חָמֵץ from our possession before פֶּסַח.

We are forbidden *to own* חָמֵץ, see our חָמֵץ in our possession or *benefit from it* in any way during פֶּסַח.

מִדְאוֹרַיְיתָא – from the תּוֹרָה שֶׁבִּכְתָב (– Written Torah Law) we can fulfill the מִצְוָה of removing the חָמֵץ by nullifying it (canceling it out) in our hearts, meaning that we decide that the חָמֵץ no longer belongs to us and is הֶפְקֵר – free for anyone to take.

Our Rabbis have established that the חָמֵץ nullification is not enough, because a person might not really nullify it with a complete heart – and deep down he may still want to keep his precious חָמֵץ. Therefore the חֲכָמִים established that we must either burn it or *physically remove it*.

Even חָמֵץ that was sold to a non Jew – as we will soon learn about – must be removed from our sight during פֶּסַח. This is because we are so used to eating חָמֵץ throughout the year, that if חָמֵץ is left around the house during פֶּסַח, then one might mistakenly just snatch and eat it, even if he nullified it in his heart and mind.

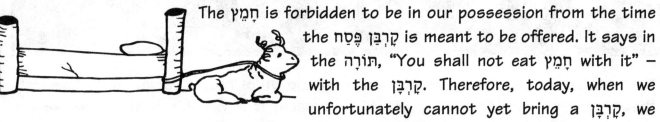
By when must the חָמֵץ be removed from our possession?

The חָמֵץ is forbidden to be in our possession from the time the קָרְבַּן פֶּסַח is meant to be offered. It says in the תּוֹרָה, "You shall not eat חָמֵץ with it" – with the קָרְבָּן. Therefore, today, when we unfortunately cannot yet bring a קָרְבָּן, we remove all the חָמֵץ from our possession the same time the קָרְבָּן would have been offered.

The קָרְבָּן was offered (at the earliest) half an hour after חֲצוֹת הַיּוֹם - mid-day of the 14th day of נִיסָן. This is the "seventh hour" of the day, as the *day* (light time) is divided into 12 parts[8].

In order to be careful, we do the "בִּיעוּר חָמֵץ" (burning of the חָמֵץ) one hour earlier, at the end of the *fifth* hour of the day. The exact time is different in each city. Please contact your local Rabbi or check your Shul's website to find out the time in your area.

We gather all the leftover חָמֵץ into a safe area, or metal can, and burn it. We say a slightly different כָּל חֲמִירָא once more, to nullify the חָמֵץ that we saved the night before, and for some of it that may have moved from the place we put it.

Why don't we say the שֶׁהֶחֱיָינוּ on the בִּיעוּר? Usually if we do something "new", or something we didn't do for a while, we say the שֶׁהֶחֱיָינוּ!?

One reason is because we say the שֶׁהֶחֱיָינוּ in the קִידוּשׁ of פֶּסַח and we have in mind all the different matters of פֶּסַח. Another reason is because we only say the שֶׁהֶחֱיָינוּ on something that we have pleasure from, or a happy occasion. Here, however, we are burning our possessions, and this is not considered a "happy occasion."

DOODLE A FIRE:

---

[8] This is a שָׁעָה זְמַנִית – a Halachic Hour – in which the daylight time is divided into 12 equal parts, and each part is one hour. The תּוֹרָה says that the קָרְבָּן needs to be brought in the 7th hour. This means the 7th hour of the day – the way it is divided the Halachic way – <u>not</u> 7:00!

SELLING THE CHAMETZ - מְכִירַת חָמֵץ

The תּוֹרָה forbids us to own any חָמֵץ during the יוֹם טוֹב of פֶּסַח. A person might have חָמֵץ that he doesn't want to burn or get rid of, because it is valuable. In this case, we are allowed to sell the חָמֵץ to a non-Jewish person before פֶּסַח. Once the time in which we are forbidden to own חָמֵץ arrives, it is already too late to sell the חָמֵץ and it must be burned, during or even after פֶּסַח.

The חָמֵץ that will be sold to a non-Jew, should be removed from our house and given to the non-Jew. If the חָמֵץ needs to stay in our home, it must be put away in a closed off area of the house. The part of the house where the חָמֵץ stays, also belongs to the non-Jew. It is not ours, so we do not enter the area, or open the cabinets during פֶּסַח.

A contract must be written up, stating that the חָמֵץ is being sold to this person, at this price. After פֶּסַח, the original Jewish owner buys back the חָמֵץ from the non-Jew.

Even if you know that the non-Jew will not want to keep your חָמֵץ, you must be *willing* to give everything away, should he want it. If you do not feel this way, then you really aren't selling the חָמֵץ, which means that you *own* חָמֵץ during פֶּסַח. This is a very serious עֲבֵירָה (sin).

The process and details of the "selling of the חָמֵץ" is not a simple one. It involves complicated matters which the "seller" and "buyer" must know. Therefore, most communities appoint a reliable Rabbi to sell the חָמֵץ for them. The Rabbi is the "representative" in the sale with the non-Jew. Some actually sell the חָמֵץ to the Rabbi, and the Rabbi sells it to the non Jew. Since the Rabbi knows all the necessary laws, we know we are safe! Our חָמֵץ will truly be out of our possession during פֶּסַח.

Even חָמֵץ that was sold to a non Jew must be <u>removed from our sight</u> during פֶּסַח. This is because a person is so used to eating חָמֵץ throughout the year, that If חָמֵץ is left around the house during פֶּסַ, then one might mistakenly eat it, even if he sold it.

Any חָמֵץ that was not sold to a non-Jew and stayed in the possession of a Jew during פֶּסַח – even by mistake – is called "חָמֵץ שֶׁעָבַר עָלָיו הַפֶּסַח" (Chometz that "passed through" the *Pesach*). This חָמֵץ is forbidden to us forever, and must be burned. This is a גְזֵירָה (decree) of the חֲכָמִים (Sages), so that people would be more careful about removing חָמֵץ from their possession.

WATCHED/GUARDED MATZAH - מַצָּה שְׁמוּרָה

> For seven days, you shall eat Matzah
> (Shemot 12:15)
>
> שִׁבְעַת יָמִים מַצּוֹת תּאֹכֵלוּ (שְׁמוֹת יב:טו)

> And you shall guard (- be careful about)
> the Matzot (Shemot 12:17)
>
> וּשְׁמַרְתֶּם אֶת הַמַּצּוֹת (שְׁמוֹת יב:יז)

The מַצָּה we use for פֶּסַח is called מַצָּה שְׁמוּרָה - *Matzah Shmurah*. What does this mean?

The word שְׁמוּרָה means "watched" or "guarded". The "careful watch" begins while the wheat is still on the field. From the time the wheat is grown, it is carefully protected against any extra contact with water, which could cause the wheat kernels to become חָמֵץ.

The wheat is actually cut a little early, before its full ripening. For, if it is totally ripe and it comes in contact with water, it can become חָמֵץ, even while it is growing!

Specially trained Rabbis travel to the wheat fields in July, and supervise the harvesting process. They bring the wheat to the flour mill which is thoroughly cleaned and carefully checked. They inspect the kernels to make sure that they have not become moist or damp. Then they watch as the wheat is ground into flour. The next step is sealing the big sacks of flour which are delivered to the מַצָּה bakery.

DOODLE YOUR FAVORITE RABBI:

The water used for the מַצָּה is called [9]"מַיִם שֶׁלָּנוּ" – "water which stayed overnight."

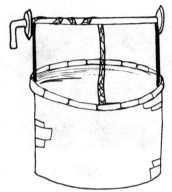

This water is drawn from a well. The one who draws the water must have in mind, that this water is being drawn for the מִצְוָה of baking מַצָּה. The drawn water is kept standing overnight, to ensure the proper temperature needed for the flour and water to mix in the very best way.

The flour and water are mixed under careful supervision. Then the dough is rushed to the kneading table. There it is kneaded, rolled and gets special מַצָּה holes put into it. The dough is worked with non-stop - on paper covered tables, until it goes into the oven. If the dough is left alone even for a short time, it starts to rise, and within 18 minutes, it can become חָמֵץ.

All the vessels that are being used for the flour and dough, including the bowls and the rolling pins, are scrubbed clean every few minutes. The paper table-covers are also changed after every batch.

The people working must have in mind and *say* the words "לְשֵׁם מַצּוֹת מִצְוָה" – "This is being done for the purpose of *Matzos* of (the) *Mitzvah*", - the Matzos that are eaten at the Seder.
For a wonderful experience... - *Visit a real Matzah bakery!*

We must make sure to keep the baked מַצּוֹת in a clean dry place too. Any contact with water, even after it was baked, might turn the מַצָּה into חָמֵץ. How? If particles of flour did not fully mix with the water earlier, and did not bake very well, this flour can start rising if it touches water. This can make it [10]חָמֵץ.

---

[9] Don't get confused with the common translation of the word שֶׁלָּנוּ – ours... this is NOT that word. Here the שֶׁרֶשׁ is לָנָה – sleeping overnight.

[10] This is one of the reasons some have a custom not to eat מַצָּה שְׁרוּיָ'ה during פֶּסַח - this is מַצָּה that was soaked or even dipped in any kind of liquid or spread that contains water. Some who don't eat מַצָּה שְׁרוּיָ'ה during פֶּסַח – do however eat it on the last day of פֶּסַח.

There are other kinds of מַצָּה that are also כָּשֵׁר לְפֶסַח, but it is best to eat only מַצָּה שְׁמוּרָה on פֶּסַח. If one cannot eat מַצָּה שְׁמוּרָה throughout the whole פֶּסַח, then at least for the סֵדֶר nights, every effort should be made to have "the real thing."

There is another kind of מַצָּה called מַצָּה עֲשִׁירָה – "rich" מַצָּה- because of its "rich" ingredients. This is מַצָּה made with fruit juice or eggs. We avoid these on פֶּסַח. If necessary these מַצּוֹת can be eaten by very young children and the elderly.

One of the reasons to avoid this מַצָּה is because when coming in contact with water, מַצּוֹת that are made with juice become חָמֵץ, even quicker than regular מַצּוֹת.

Some say that people should avoid machine made מַצָּה for a few reasons:

• מַצָּה must be made with the כַּוָּנָה (intent, and purpose) of making the מַצּוֹת מִצְוָה, and machines do not have minds!

• There are so many parts to a machine, there might be a part that is very hard to clean, and some dough could be left over there for more than 18 minutes...

• If some of the parts of the machine become too hot, it could make the dough rise early.

• The 18 minute time frame that we were given concerning the baking of the מַצָּה was decided on hand made מַצּוֹת. The necessary time for machine made מַצּוֹת might be different.

עֶרֶב פֶּסַח - EREV PESACH

The 14th of נִיסָן, the day before פֶּסַח is called עֶרֶב פֶּסַח [11].

It is one of the busiest days of the year!

By this time there is no חָמֵץ left in our homes, and all our efforts are focused on preparing for פֶּסַח and specifically for the סֵדֶר.

Most people remember the flowing tears whilst preparing the מָרוֹר...

There are (oh so) many different customs in the way people celebrate פֶּסַח, and in the foods that are eaten. Some people are so strict on פֶּסַח that they do not eat anything that was processed in a factory[12]. They eat only מַצָּה, chicken / meat, fruits and vegetables. They eat only כָּשֵׁר Kosher for פֶּסַח cakes or cookies that were baked at home, and drink only drinks that were made at home.

For these people, עֶרֶב פֶּסַח is especially busy. They spend many hours preparing the food and drinks. They squeeze their own oranges for orange juice, and lemons for lemon juice.

Some people have the custom not to eat קִטְנִיוֹת on פֶּסַח. These are foods that look like flour when they are ground. They include rice, beans peas and peanuts, millet and other similar grains. Generally, אַשְׁכְּנַזִים do not eat קִטְנִיוֹת while סְפָרָדִים do.

עֶרֶב פֶּסַח is a fast-day for the firstborn boys and men in the family. They fast to thank ה' for saving them when all the בְּכוֹרֵי מִצְרַיִם were killed. The בְּכוֹרוֹת usually partake in a סִיוּם (when one completes learning a book of Mishna or Talmud,) which includes a סְעוּדַת מִצְוָה – a feast of Mitzvah. This enables them to eat even on their fast day.

On עֶרֶב פֶּסַח after מִנְחָה we say the סֵדֶר קָרְבַּן פֶּסַח (process of how the Pesach sacrifice was offered). We would really like to bring the real קָרְבָּן, but we aren't allowed to, we therefore read about it, as if to tell ה' "please accept our תְּפִילָה as if we had really offered the קָרְבָּן."

As we mentioned the קָרְבָּן פֶּסַח, lets learn a little about it, and how it is connected to our יום טוב!

---

[11] The day before any יום טוב is called "עֶרֶב יוֹם טוֹב".

[12] The simple idea here is that they want to be 100% sure that they are not eating חָמֵץ on פֶּסַח. If they make everything at home, they need not worry if someone at the factory dropped a crumb of his lunch into the food or drink.

THE קָרְבָּן WAY...

On the 10th of this month every man must take for himself a lamb for each family a lamb for each household *(Shemot 12:3)*	...בֶּעָשׂר לַחֹדֶשׁ הַזֶּה וְיִקְחוּ לָהֶם אִישׁ שֶׂה לְבֵית אָבֹת שֶׂה לַבָּיִת (שמות יב:ג)
And you should hold it in safekeeping until the 14th day of this month	וְהָיָה לָכֶם לְמִשְׁמֶרֶת עַד אַרְבָּעָה עָשָׂר יוֹם לַחֹדֶשׁ הַזֶּה
And the whole community of Israel shall slaughter it in the afternoon *(Shemot 12:6)*	וְשָׁחֲטוּ אֹתוֹ כֹּל קְהַל עֲדַת יִשְׂרָאֵל בֵּין הָעַרְבָּיִם (שמות יב:ו...)
And they should eat the meat on this night	וְאָכְלוּ אֶת הַבָּשָׂר בַּלַּיְלָה הַזֶּה
Eat it roasted by fire – together with Matzot and Maror	צְלִי אֵשׁ וּמַצּוֹת עַל מְרֹרִים יֹאכְלֻהוּ
Do not eat it rare (partially roasted) or cooked in water	אַל תֹּאכְלוּ מִמֶּנּוּ נָא וּבָשֵׁל מְבֻשָּׁל בַּמָּיִם
But only roasted by fire	כִּי אִם צְלִי אֵשׁ
Do not leave any of it for the next morning, and whatever remains until morning you shall burn in fire.	וְלֹא תוֹתִירוּ מִמֶּנּוּ עַד בֹּקֶר וְהַנֹּתָר מִמֶּנּוּ עַד בֹּקֶר בָּאֵשׁ תִּשְׂרֹפוּ
It should be eaten in one house Do not take any of the meat out of the house and do not break any bones in it *(Shemot 12:46)*	בְּבַיִת אֶחָד יֵאָכֵל לֹא-תוֹצִיא מִן הַבַּיִת מִן הַבָּשָׂר חוּצָה וְעֶצֶם לֹא תִשְׁבְּרוּ בוֹ (שמות יב:מו)
And you should not keep the sacrifice overnight – until the morning *(Shemot 34: 25)*	וְלֹא יָלִין לַבֹּקֶר זֶבַח חַג הַפָּסַח (שמות לד:כה)

In the times of the בֵּית הַמִּקְדָּשׁ when the קָרְבָּן פֶּסַח was offered, people would gather together in groups, and partake in the סְעוּדָה – the festive meal, eating from the animal they sacrificed as desert.

The תּוֹרָה tells us many laws concerning the way it had to be brought, and eaten.

Sefer HaChinuch explains in a very interesting way, how the laws of קָרְבָּן פֶּסַח symbolize royalty. Here are a few examples:

THE קָרְבָּן WAY...	THE ROYAL WAY...
It was forbidden to bring and share any part of it outside of the group.	Imagine a group of kings living next to each other. When they have their meals, they do not have to "share" with each other, because each one has more than what he needs!
The קָרְבָּן פֶּסַח had too be roasted, not cooked.	When you cook meat in water, you get "more" to eat, than when you roast it. In those days the poor people would cook their meat, the rich would roast it.
It was forbidden to break any bone it the meat – even while chewing it.	Breaking the bones and chewing them, also used to be a "poor man's thing to do." The rich never "had to" chew the bones, they always had enough. The poor would try to "get every bit" of the meat, and chew the bones.
It was forbidden to leave any part of the meat over until the next day, and if one did, it had to be burned.	A poor person has to leave over food from one day to the next. A rich and royal household will cook fresh for the next day, and throw out the leftovers.

ERUV TAVSHILIN – עֵירוּב תַּבְשִׁילִין

On שַׁבָּת and יוֹם טוֹב we are not allowed to do any work in preparation for another day.

When any יוֹם טוֹב falls on a Friday & Shabbat or Thursday & Friday – we have a challenge:

We are never allowed to cook on שַׁבָּת, and we are forbidden to prepare on יוֹם טוֹב - even for such a holy day as שַׁבָּת.

So how will we be able to eat on שַׁבָּת when we cannot prepare the day before?

(מִדְּאוֹרַיְיתָא - If the food was cooked while there was enough time to eat it before שַׁבָּת comes – it is ok.)

The רַבָּנָן arranged a solution: we make an עֵירוּב תַּבְשִׁילִין - which allows one to cook on יוֹם טוֹב for שַׁבָּת.

This מִצְוָה is one of the שֶׁבַע מִצְוֹת דְּרַבָּנָן – the seven מִצְוֹת that are not written in the תּוֹרָה but were established by the רַבָּנָן. (We also make בְּרָכוֹת on these מִצְוֹת.)

What do we do?

On עֶרֶב יוֹם טוֹב we take two foods:

- One portion of מַצָּה - minimum size "kibaitzah" like the size of an egg.
- One cooked portion, like fish or meat, minimum size "kizayit" size of an olive.

We hold them in our hands – as if to say that this is the beginning of the preparation of the שַׁבָּת food – and because we started the שַׁבָּת preparation now – before יוֹם טוֹב, we may continue the baking and cooking (for שַׁבָּת) on יוֹם טוֹב too.

While holding the food we say the בְּרָכָה:

בָּא״י אֱמֶ״הָ אקב״ן עַל מִצְוַת עֵירוּב

Then we say another paragraph that explains the idea of the עֵירוּב –that because of this we are allowed to bake and cook for שַׁבָּת.

Every household must have their own עֵירוּב תַּבְשִׁילִין.

Nevertheless, the Rabbi of the city[13] always makes the עֵירוּב תַּבְשִׁילִין for the others in that city who did not make an עֵירוּב.

The people that did not make their own עֵירוּב תַּבְשִׁילִין, - either because they couldn't, or because they do not know the הֲלָכָה, - will be יוֹצֵא (fulfill their obligation) through the Rabbi's עֵירוּב תַּבְשִׁילִין. If one knows the הֲלָכָה and was lazy to make the עֵירוּב or forgot... s/he is not יוֹצֵא the Rabbi's עֵירוּב and is not allowed to bake or cook on יוֹם טוֹב in preparation for שַׁבָּת. (If this should happen, make sure to ask your local Rav what to do.)

Our Rabbis give two reasons for the עֵירוּב תַּבְשִׁילִין.

One for כְּבוֹד שַׁבָּת, one for כְּבוֹד יוֹם טוֹב:

כְּבוֹד שַׁבָּת: - this strengthens our respect for שַׁבָּת. How?

If we must prepare for שַׁבָּת even before יוֹם טוֹב starts, we will take the time to think about other things we may need for שַׁבָּת and prepare special foods for שַׁבָּת now, when we can – before יוֹם טוֹב begins.

כְּבוֹד יוֹם טוֹב: - this strengthens our honor for יוֹם טוֹב – because when we see that we cannot prepare on יוֹם טוֹב even for such a holy day like שַׁבָּת – then surely we cannot prepare on יוֹם טוֹב for a "regular" day.

---

[13] And anyone else that wants to may do the same – but there is a "process" that needs to be done – as is explained in the שלחן ערוך.

הַדְלָקַת הַנֵרוֹת – CANDLE LIGHTING

On יד נִיסָן in the evening before sunset, we light the יום טוב candles.

WHAT	HOW	WHY
We light יום טוב candles 	Women and girls light the יום טוב candles before sunset. The בְּרָכוֹת we say are: בָּא"י אֱמֶ"הָ אקב"ן לְהַדְלִיק נֵר שֶׁל יום טוב (If יום טוב falls on שַׁבָּת, then the בְּרָכָה is: בָּא"י אֱמֶ"הָ אקב"ן לְהַדליק נֵר שֶׁל שַׁבָּת וְשֶׁל יום טוב) We then say the special בְּרָכָה thanking Hashem for keeping us alive and healthy to celebrate this occasion: בָּא"י אֱמֶ"הָ שֶׁהֶחֱיָינוּ וְקִיְּמָנוּ וְהִגִּיעָנוּ לִזְמַן הַזֶּה On the *second night*, the candles are lit *after three stars* appear. We should also light these candles from a *fire that was already burning* during יום טוב. We are not allowed to create a new fire on יום טוב.	To honor the day, we light candles for it. Also, it adds peace in the home, when we light candles for שַׁבָּת and יום טוב. We wait until nightfall on the second night, because we are not allowed to prepare on one day of יום טוב for the next. 

THE סֵדֶר PLATE

For the סֵדֶר, we prepare <u>three</u> מַצּוֹת, one on top of the next. Here are a few reasons:

WHAT	WHY
We prepare three מַצּוֹת for the סֵדֶר plate 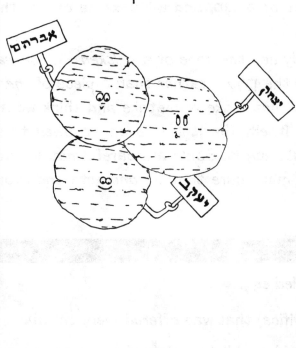	1. The main reason is because we need two מַצּוֹת for the usual לֶחֶם מִשְׁנֶה (double loaf) that we have every שַׁבָּת and יוֹם טוֹב. The third מַצָּה is the לֶחֶם עוֹנִי - bread of affliction/suffering/poverty (of poor people), specifically for the Seder night. 2. The three מַצּוֹת symbolize the three categories of בְּנֵי יִשְׂרָאֵל: ➤ כֹּהֵן ➤ לֵוִי ➤ יִשְׂרָאֵל 3. The three מַצּוֹת symbolize the three אָבוֹת: ➤ אַבְרָהָם ➤ יִצְחָק ➤ יַעֲקֹב

The סֵדֶר plate itself is called the קְעָרָה (*bowl*). It has six things on it, and is set up in the following way. Like the spikes?

בֵּיצָה

זְרוֹעַ

מָרוֹר

כַּרְפַּס

חֲרֹסֶת

חֲזֶרֶת

זְרוֹעַ Zero'ah

A piece of roasted meat: Usually the neck of a chicken, or a shank bone.

This represents the קָרְבַּן פֶּסַח (*Pesach* offering). It is called the "זְרוֹעַ" from the words: "בְּיָד חֲזָקָה וּבִזְרוֹעַ נְטוּיָה". This refers to 'ה's "outstretched arm" with which He took us out of מִצְרַיִם, and will take us out of this גָלוּת (Exile).

We specifically use the bone of a *chicken* – which was not offered for the קָרְבָּן – rather than a piece of *meat*, so that one should not make a mistake and think we are "offering" the קָרְבַּן פֶּסַח itself. The קָרְבָּן was only allowed to be offered in יְרוּשָׁלַיִם. Now, we are only remembering it. Some are careful not to even touch the chicken bone during the סֵדֶר, to make sure that no-one gets the wrong idea.

בֵּיצָה Beitzah

A hard boiled egg.

This represents the קָרְבַּן חֲגִיגָה (Festival sacrifice) that was offered every יוֹם טוֹב.

An egg is used here, because the egg is round, and it is a sign of our mourning over the destruction of the בֵּית הַמִּקְדָּשׁ.

Another "egg message": It is round without any opening. This is as if we are asking 'ה that whoever wants to even say something bad about the Jews, should not be able to, just like the egg that has no opening and cannot speak.

The roundness of the egg also tells us that the "Wheel Of Destiny" turns, and even though we are now in גָלוּת, we will surely soon be redeemed.

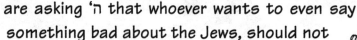

בס"ד

PESACH

פֶּסַח

Maror מָרוֹר

Bitter Herbs: Usually horseradish and/or romaine lettuce.

To remember
the hard and bitter work
the Jews were forced to do
for the Egyptians.

Charoset חֲרוֹסֶת

A mixture of grated apples, nuts and red wine. Other fruits, and spices are sometimes added (i.e. dates, pears, cinnamon etc.).

This resembles the cement בְּנֵי יִשְׂרָאֵל were forced to make.

The ingredients are all related to the story too.

The apples – because the Jewish women in מִצְרַיִם would give birth in the fields under the thick shade of the apple tree. (They feared that if the מִצְרִים would see their babies, they wouldn't have a chance to live.)

The red wine – symbolizes the blood of the מִילָה (circumcision) and the קָרְבַּן פֶּסַח.

The nuts – in Hebrew שְׁקֵדִים, which can also be translated to שְׁקִידָה (speed).

This is to remember how 'ה took us swiftly out of מִצְרַיִם.

The cinnamon – before it's ground, looks like straw, which our forefathers used to build the bricks in מִצְרַיִם.

Karpas כַּרְפַּס

A vegetable: Most commonly a boiled potato, onion, parsley, celery or radish.

The vegetable will be dipped into saltwater, to remember the tears that were shed in מִצְרַיִם.

If you reverse the (Hebrew) letters of the word כַּרְפַּס, you get "פֶּרֶך ס'" The גְמַטְרִיָא of ס' = 60. The number 60 is short for and refers to the 600,000 Jews who were slaves, and did "פֶּרֶך" – backbreaking work in מִצְרַיִם.

Chazeres חֲזֶרֶת

Romaine lettuce: This is considered a kind of מָרוֹר.

This is used for the sandwich of כּוֹרֵך – the tenth part of the סֵדֶר, when we "sandwich" the מַצָה and מָרוֹר.

Romaine lettuce is used, because at first, as it grows and becomes ripe it is sweet, then as time goes on it becomes more and more bitter. The same idea happened with our forefathers in מִצְרַיִם. In the beginning, פַּרְעֹה paid them to do work for him, later he stopped paying and forced them to continue as slaves.

Place the Seder Plate items inside their plates.

THE FOUR CUPS – ד' כּוֹסוֹת

During the סֵדֶר we drink four cups of wine. Why <u>four</u>?
Each of the "Four Cups" of wine have their own purpose:

Cup # 1 - is for קִידוּש, which we make every שַׁבָּת and יוֹם טוֹב.

Cup # 2 - is honors the הַגָּדָה, and we drink it after we read the הַגָּדָה.

Cup # 3 - is for בִּרְכַּת הַמָּזוֹן – the *Bentching*. This cup we also drink on שַׁבָּת and יוֹם טוֹב.

Cup # 4 - is connected to הַלֵּל – the praise we say to ה', while we ask Him for מָשִׁיחַ.

A few other reasons:

- According to the *Maharal*, just as the 3 מַצוֹת represent the 3 אָבוֹת, the four cups represent the four אִמָהוֹת:

שָׂרָה   רִבְקָה   רָחֵל   לֵאָה

- According to the *Abarbanel*, there are four "central" גְּאוּלוֹת (redemptions). They are:

1. ה' chose us, beginning with אַבְרָהָם, to be His Nation.
2. The redemption from מִצְרַיִם.
3. The fact that the Jewish People still exist in this גָלוּת.
4. The future Redemption, with מָשִׁיחַ.

The most famous reason for the 4 cups is[14]:

In פֶּרֶק ו שְׁמוֹת the ה' talks about taking בְּנֵי יִשְׂרָאֵל out of מִצְרַיִם, He uses the famous "Four expressions of Redemption:"

Therefore say to the Children of Israel "I am Hashem"	לָכֵן אֱמֹר לִבְנֵי-יִשְׂרָאֵל אֲנִי ה'
and I will take you (out) away from your forced labor in Egypt	וְהוֹצֵאתִי אֶתְכֶם מִתַּחַת סִבְלֹת מִצְרַיִם
and I will save you from their work	וְהִצַּלְתִּי אֶתְכֶם מֵעֲבֹדָתָם
and I will redeem you with an outstretched arm and with great acts of judgments	וְגָאַלְתִּי אֶתְכֶם בִּזְרוֹעַ נְטוּיָה וּבִשְׁפָטִים גְּדֹלִים
and I will take you to Myself as a Nation – and I will be to you as a G-D	וְלָקַחְתִּי אֶתְכֶם לִי לְעָם וְהָיִיתִי לָכֶם לֵא-לֹקִים
And I will bring you into the land... (Shemot 6: 6-8)	וְהֵבֵאתִי אֶתְכֶם אֶל-הָאָרֶץ... (שמות ו:ו-ח)

The first four expressions of גְּאֻלָה (redemption) talk about ה' taking us out of מִצְרַיִם.

And I will bring you out...	וְהוֹצֵאתִי אֶתְכֶם
And I will save you...	וְהִצַּלְתִּי אֶתְכֶם
And I will redeem you...	וְגָאַלְתִּי אֶתְכֶם
And I will take you...	וְלָקַחְתִּי אֶתְכֶם

We drink one cup for each of these special expressions.

The fifth expression "וְהֵבֵאתִי" – And I will bring you into the land... also reminds us of the future - and for this we have the "fifth cup" the cup of אֵלִיָהוּ הַנָבִיא.

Can you repeat the 4 expressions by heart yet?

[14] The *Midrash* says that the four cups represent the four decrees which פַּרְעֹה issued against the Jews, and the four ways which the Jew kept themselves separate from the Egyptians. The four cups also correspond to the four times that פַּרְעֹה's cup is mentioned in his dream that יוֹסֵף interpreted.

Quick Chart:

CUP #	REASON #1	REASON #2	REASON #3	REASON #4
❶	קִידוּשׁ	שָׂרָה	בְּחִירַת אַבְרָהָם	וְהוֹצֵאתִי
❷	הַגָּדָה	רִבְקָה	גְּאוּלַת מִצְרַיִם	וְהִצַּלְתִּי
❸	בִּרְכַּת הַמָּזוֹן	רָחֵל	קִיּוּם בְּנֵי יִשְׂרָאֵל	וְגָאַלְתִּי
❹	הַלֵּל	לֵאָה	מָשִׁיחַ	וְלָקַחְתִּי

We know, that before we do a מִצְוָה, we make a בְּרָכָה. For example, before we put on תְּפִילִין, we make a בְּרָכָה, before we light שַׁבָּת candles, we make a בְּרָכָה. Before we learn תּוֹרָה, as we put on our צִיצַת we make a בְּרָכָה and there are so many more.

Why then, don't we make a בְּרָכָה before we begin the מִצְוָה of drinking the four cups of wine? – Perhaps... אֲקַבְּ"ן עַל שְׁתִיַּית ד' כּוֹסוֹת...

One reason is: Since we don't drink them all together, we are not completing the מִצְוָה at the time of the בְּרָכָה, and when we make a בְּרָכָה on something, we should finish the מִצְוָה.

Another reason is: When people drink wine, it usually has an effect.... It is imaginable, that someone might drink one cup of wine, then another, then another, and - if the wine is strong enough.... - he might be too drunk to even remember that there is a fourth! If one would make a בְּרָכָה on the "4 cups" and not finish all four, it would be a בְּרָכָה לְבַטָּלָה – a Blessing in vein!

The color of the wine should be red, symbolizing:

➤ The blood of the קָרְבַּן פֶּסַח – the *Pesach* Sacrifice.

➤ The blood of the מִילָה - the circumcision.

In the זְכוּת – merit – of these two מִצְווֹת, בְּנֵי יִשְׂרָאֵל were freed from מִצְרַיִם. At the time of the גְּאוּלָה when בְּנֵי יִשְׂרָאֵל were supposed to leave מִצְרַיִם, they did not have enough merits to be redeemed, so, in His kindness, ה' gave them 2 more מִצְווֹת to fulfill, the קָרְבַּן פֶּסַח and the בְּרִית. This made them worthy of the גְּאוּלָה – redemption.

• Other reasons for the wine to be red:

• Symbolizing the blood that בְּנֵי יִשְׂרָאֵל sprinkled on their doorposts in מִצְרַיִם.

• Symbolizing the Jewish children's blood in which the wicked king פַּרְעֹה would bathe.

THE סֶדֶר – *SEDER* – ORDER OF THE NIGHT

What *do* we do on פֶּסַח night? We have a סֶדֶר of course! What does *that* mean? We sit down to a festive meal, and do lots of different things.

Some of which seem pretty strange to the untrained eye...

One of the main מִצְוֹת of פֶּסַח is " וְהִגַּדְתָּ לְבִנְךָ – tell it to your son (your children)" which means that parents have the obligation to tell their children about all the wonders and miracles of the story of יְצִיאַת מִצְרַיִם.

The סֶדֶר together with all the interesting things that we do, usually takes quite a few hours. It sometime continues until the wee hours of the morning. The "problem" is that children might fall asleep before it is over, and the סֶדֶר really is *mainly for the children*!

Therefore, our חֲכָמִים established that we do a few things during the סֶדֶר that will help keep the children awake. These are unusual things, that the child doesn't see happen during the year. The child will then be curious and ask "Why is this night different from all other nights of the year....?" The child will then ask about all the interesting things that are happening, and will stay awake.

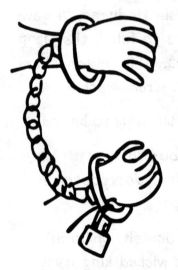

This also gives the parents the opportunity to answer the child's question, by telling the child the reason for this סֶדֶר. "...Long, long ago, מִצְרַיִם in פַּרְעֹה to slaves were we – עֲבָדִים הָיִינוּ, and ה' took us out with a strong hand....!"

You will also notice that during our סֶדֶר we do seemingly contradictory (opposite) things. We recline towards our left side while we eat, as that is the custom of Kings, a sign of royalty and freedom, and we also eat the bitter מָרוֹר as a sign of slavery!

These opposite feelings are expressed throughout the סֶדֶר, because on this night, we remember both our slavery in מִצְרַיִם, and our freedom and redemption from מִצְרַיִם. For, in order to really appreciate our freedom, we need to remember our slavery. Therefore we do many things that represent freedom and others that symbolize slavery.

On a deeper level:

The real question is *not* "Why do we do opposite things during our סֵדֶר." The question is a much stronger one:

When we celebrate a יוֹם טוֹב, we are not supposed to "just *do* some things to *remember* what happened many years ago." We need to "*live*" and *experience* the message of that יוֹם טוֹב.

The message of פֶּסַח is freedom from גָלוּת.

When we celebrate it now, however, how can we truly relive and experience freedom from גָלוּת, when we *still are* in גָלוּת?!

The Seder teaches us that the freedom of slavery in מִצְרַיִם was not the complete and true redemption of the Jewish People – if it was, we would never be in גָלוּת again... יְצִיאַת מִצְרַיִם was really the *beginning of the process* of the true גְאוּלָה. The completion of the Jewish People's redemption will take place when מָשִׁיחַ comes, and brings us all into אֶרֶץ יִשְׂרָאֵל, and rebuilds the בֵּית הַמִקְדָשׁ.

יְצִיאַת מִצְרַיִם was the initiation (starting) of the process of the real and ultimate גְאוּלָה. What happened at יְצִיאַת מִצְרַיִם gave us the power to come to the real and everlasting גְאוּלָה.

We see this throughout the סֵדֶר. We do things that symbolize freedom, to celebrate what happened to us בַּיָמִים הָהֵם בַּזְמַן הַזֶה – in those days, at this time", the גְאוּלָה that was the beginning of the everlasting גְאוּלָה.

We do other things that symbolize slavery, to know and remember that we are still in גָלוּת, and we still need the גְאוּלָה. We ask ה׳ in our תְּפִילוֹת during the סֵדֶר, to lead us to the true and complete redemption.

THE *SEDER* SIGNS - סִימָנֵי הַסֵדֶר

בָּרֵךְ	מָרוֹר	מַגִיד	קַדֵשׁ
הַלֵל	כּוֹרֵךְ	רָחְצָה	וּרְחַץ
נִרְצָה	שֻׁלְחָן עוֹרֵךְ	מוֹצִיא	כַּרְפַּס
	צָפוּן	מַצָה	יַחַץ

THE SEDER SIGNS – סִימָנֵי הַסֵּדֶר

The word סֵדֶר means *order*. Since there are so many important laws and customs regarding the סֵדֶר פֶּסַח, our חֲכָמִים organized the סֵדֶר in a very orderly 15 steps. They also gave us 15 signs to help us remember the "order" of the סֵדֶר. These signs are called the "סִימָנֵי הַסֵּדֶר" – the signs of the Seder. Here are the signs and their explanations.

קַדֵּשׁ
Kadesh

Kiddush

We make קִידוּשׁ *on wine,* just as we do on every שַׁבָּת and יוֹם טוֹב, to honor the day and make it holy.

Usually, on a regular שַׁבָּת or יוֹם טוֹב, the קִידוּשׁ can be made as early in the day as one wants. On פֶּסַח however, we must wait until night time, when the stars come out. However, we make the קִידוּשׁ immediately, when we can, so that even the young children could participate.

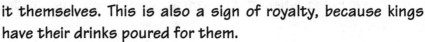

Some have the custom, that for all four cups, every person should have their wine poured into their cup by someone else, and not pour it themselves. This is also a sign of royalty, because kings have their drinks poured for them.

This is the first cup of the four cups. We drink the *entire cup* reclining towards our left side (leaning on a pillow if possible) as a symbol of freedom. (If one cannot drink the whole cup, then an effort should be made to drink most of it).

Pesach:

Our Journey

to Freedom

KADESH: Translation 1. Separate, Rise above 2. Sanctify - make holy

The beginning of all journeys is actually walking out the door. You've got to leave somewhere to go somewhere else. It is also the first step towards freedom: We ignore the voice of our internal Pharaoh/Yetzer Harah inside that mocks us, and tries to keep us in the same spiritual place by saying, "Who are you to even begin such a transformative journey?"

Step one is leave. Just get up and rise above your current condition.

This is the first meaning of the word, "Kadesh" - to *rise above / leave* our current condition. Then we are ready for the second meaning: Once we've set ourselves free, we've got the power to transform and sanctify a similar situation, to make it a holy one.

When we take real steps to being better, less selfish and more selfless – we have begun our Journey to Personal Freedom.

וּרְחַץ
Urechatz

Washing hands

We wash our hands.

During the times of the בֵּית הַמִּקְדָּש, the custom was that when someone ate something dipped in water, he would wash his hands the very same way we do for bread - without saying the בְּרָכָה for washing – עַל נְטִילַת יָדַיִם. The reason for this washing is because food that came into contact with water is מוּכְשָׁר לְקַבֵּל טוּמְאָה – could become טָמֵא – impure. We wash our hands to purify ourselves before we touch the wet food.

Today, not all people are careful about this custom (although we all should... and some still are...) but on the night of the סֵדֶר we all follow this custom. One of the reasons for this is, to arouse children's curiosity so they will ask *"Why?"*

Pesach:
Our Journey
to Freedom

URCHATZ: Washing our hands.

We use our hands to hug, to work, to play, and sometimes G-d forbid, for no good.

Our hands obey our feelings. You love your Mom - you'll reach out and hug her. Angry at someone? You may lash out at him.

It's our mind's job to control our emotions and tell us when to back off, cool down or go ahead and hug it out.

But sometimes the mind sees one way, while the heart feels another way, and we end up doing what the heart wants, instead of what the mind knows.

Water represents the healing power of wisdom, our mind's power to control our feelings. Water flows downward, carrying its life-giving power to each thing, helping it grow. We pour water over our hands to symbolize our own mind's wisdom pouring downward, passing through our heart, thoughts and feelings and then on to our body – our actions.

When we direct our feelings to feel only good about others and to dismiss any negative thoughts - we are on our way to letting our Neshama shine. Good going! Keep it up!

כַּרְפַּס
Karpas

The Dipping

Now we take a small piece of a vegetable, usually a potato or onion, (smaller than a כְּזַיִת – an olive – so that we shouldn't have to make a בְּרָכָה אַחֲרוֹנָה on it,) and dip it into salt-water. We make the בְּרָכָה of בּוֹרֵא פְּרִי הָאֲדָמָה, and we eat it, *without* reclining.

Why this custom? In the olden days and even today, banquets begin with "appetizers" or "Entrées" – a vegetable with a dip. The custom was kept as a sign of our freedom, and mainly, to arouse children's curiosity, that they should ask "*Why is this night different...!?*"

The dipping into *salt water* is to remember our slavery.

If we reverse the name כַּרְפַּס, we get ס' פֶּרֶךְ. The ס is number 60, which refers to the 600,000 Jews in מִצְרַיִם, and פֶּרֶךְ means "back breaking labor."

When we make the בְּרָכָה for the vegetable, we have in mind that this בְּרָכָה should also apply for the מָרוֹר which we will be eating soon. (If one forgets to keep this in mind, he still does not make a בְּרָכָה on the מָרוֹר.)

We don't make a בְּרָכָה for the dipping itself, because a בְּרָכָה is only said when we do a מִצְוָה, and this is a מִנְהָג (custom) not a מִצְוָה.

Pesach:
Our Journey
to Freedom

KARPAS: Remembering the bitterness

Sometimes we need to taste the back-breaking, soul-crushing labor of Egypt to free ourselves from it once again. Our years in slavery prepared us for freedom by making us humble and able to accept Hashem's wisdom.

Being humble means realizing that "I am not the most important thing in this world, and I don't need to get my way all the time." It means recognizing that "I was created by Hashem just like everyone else – and all other creatures and insects, plants and minerals. Hashem put me here in this world for a reason. And I'd better get to it..."

How can we become humble today without slavery and suffering?

Look up at the stars above. Gaze at the marvelous world around you. When we realize how small we are relative to this great world Hashem created, and the creation of this world is such an insignificant, tiny part of what Hashem can do, we can become humble.

We are on Stop #3 of our Personal Spiritual Journey to Freedom!
Keep on truckin'!

יַחַץ Yachatz	The Split	*We break the middle* מַצָּה into two uneven parts (one bigger than the other). The bigger piece we put away for the [15] אֲפִיקוֹמָן – *Afikoman*. We put the smaller half back between the two מַצּוֹת.

(Some have the custom to hide the אֲפִיקוֹמָן from the children... Why? When you reach the אֲפִיקוֹמָן section you will see!)

The מַצָּה is called לֶחֶם עוֹנִי "the bread of affliction or poverty" or "the poor bread", reminding us of the hard times in מִצְרַיִם.

The Hebrew word "עוֹנִי" can also mean to "answer." The word עוֹנִי also has the same גְמַטְרִיָא (numerical value) as קוֹל – voice. Our חֲכָמִים explain that the מַצָּה is "The bread over which many things are said (answered)." This means that the *next* part of the הַגָּדָה and our סֵדֶר, which is מַגִּיד, must be said when the מַצָּה is before us, and we say the הַגָּדָה "over" the broken piece.

Why do we *break* the מַצָּה? One reason is because if a poor man gets a loaf of bread, he does not put the complete loaf on his table. He puts some away for the next meal, since he is not sure if he will find more food. That is also why we put away the larger piece. The poor man will try to save as much as possible for later, just in case he will need it.

This is the "bread of poverty" over which ...

Pesach:

Our Journey

to Freedom

YACHATZ: Broken Matzah - True Humility

Yachatz is another stop on Humility Road.

Matzah is called the poor man's bread. He is low and broken. And it is this brokenness that allows him to open his soul and escape his Egypt.

As long as we feel whole and complete, there is no room left for us to grow. The broken Matzah lets us realize how small we are in this big world, that we need Hashem's help – and the help of others around us, that we are not perfect. When we come to this conclusion - miracles begin in our lives.

Humility brings us to the place where we can actually start to feel Hashem in our lives, because we made room for Him.

So move over, and invite Hashem to help you drive. Now we are *really* going places!

---

[15] Some break the אֲפִיקוֹמָן into 5 pieces.

מַגִּיד	Story	*We say the* הַגָּדָה – *Haggadah.* From הָא לַחְמָא עַנְיָא until גָּאל יִשְׂרָאֵל.
Maggid	Time	

The word הַגָּדָה which means "telling" comes from the פָּסוּק in the תּוֹרָה which says "וְהִגַּדְתָּ לְבִנְךָ..." "And you should tell your child."

This is the commandment to parents, to tell, talk about and remember the story of our Exodus from מִצְרַיִם.

The תּוֹרָה tells us that we must remember יְצִיאַת מִצְרַיִם every day of the year. On פֶּסַח however, we must *talk* about it and *tell* it to others.

If מַגִּיד – the telling of the story and reading the הַגָּדָה is a מִצְוָה, why don't we make a בְּרָכָה "on reading the הַגָּדָה?!"

Some say that we are יוֹצֵא (fulfill our obligation of this מִצְוָה) through the תְּפִילָה (Davening) and קִידוּשׁ and therefore we don't need another בְּרָכָה.

A few other answers are:

❖ At the end of the הַגָּדָה, there is a בְּרָכָה which is connected to the story, "אֲשֶׁר גָּאַל..." – and that serves as the בְּרָכָה for מַגִּיד.

❖ The הַגָּדָה itself is "praise to ה'" which is really the same thing as a בְּרָכָה, therefore we don't *need* to say another בְּרָכָה.

❖ In order to make a בְּרָכָה, the מִצְוָה has to be clearly "defined" – you start here and end there. The מִצְוָה of מַגִּיד however, has no limit. One can tell the story for just a little bit, and another can continue all night long!

❖ The *Rosh* explains that the הַגָּדָה is an *answer* to the *questions* of the child, therefore it is not a מִצְוָה on its own, so it cannot have a בְּרָכָה.

We lift up the plate with the מַצּוֹת and say...

מַגִּיד Maggid	הָא לַחְמָא עַנְיָא	"*This is the bread of affliction/suffering/poverty*" over which the הַגָּדָה is said. The הַגָּדָה must be said at the time when (the Korban)"*Pesach, Matzah and Maror*" are before us. Today however, since we cannot yet fulfill the real מִצְוָה of פֶּסַח - the קָרְבַּן פֶּסַח, until the בֵּית הַמִּקְדָּשׁ is rebuilt, we have the זְרוֹעַ on the Seder Plate to symbolize the קָרְבַּן. מִדְאוֹרַיְיתָא - according to the תּוֹרָה Law - the מָרוֹר <u>must</u> be eaten *together with* the קָרְבָּן. So today without the קָרְבָּן, the מִצְוָה of מָרוֹר is מִדְרַבָּנָן – a Rabbinical מִצְוָה. Therefore, the only מִצְוָה that we fulfill מִדְאוֹרַיְיתָא – is the מַצָּה. This is why we say the הַגָּדָה <u>over the מַצָּה</u>. מַצָּה is called לֶחֶם עוֹנִי – bread of affliction & poverty, or the poor man's bread. Some say that while we were slaves in מִצְרַיִם we also ate מַצָּה, or something similar. This is the kind of food poor people eat, a broken piece, hard to digest, and very filling. Another explanation to the name לֶחֶם עוֹנִי is "לֶחֶם שֶׁעוֹנִין עָלָיו דְּבָרִים הַרְבֵּה" – bread over which many things are said (/answered). This is also hinted in the common גַּמַטְרִיָּא of עוֹנִי and קוֹל – voice - both of which are 136.
	כָּל דִכְפִין...	*Whoever is hungry let him come and eat...*" The simple meaning here is that we are inviting the hungry to join us for the Seder. However... Does it really make sense to invite people *now*?! Shouldn't that be done before we sit down to our meal...? Maybe in *Shul*, better yet - before the יוֹם טוֹב begins, but now, at the table?! Will *anybody hear* us and come? The time to truly invite people to our סֵדֶר is obviously earlier than this. By "inviting others" to our סֵדֶר now, we are really asking ה' to bring מָשִׁיחַ! (How is this, you ask! Read on!)
		In the times of the בֵּית הַמִּקְדָּשׁ, we were <u>not allowed</u> to invite just

		anyone over to our home on the סֵדֶר night. Only the family and the ones who had previously joined the קָרְבָּן "group" were allowed to participate.
		This may not seem like such a nice thing... it is, however wonderful. Because at that time, nobody was left alone without a family. Everyone had their own place to be where they fit right in!.
		Today, however, we are able to invite guests to our סֵדֶר. This is only because there is no בֵּית הַמִּקְדָּשׁ, and we cannot offer the קָרְבָּנוֹת!
		So, when we say כָּל דִכְפִין, and "invite" people, what we are really doing is saying "'ה! Look! We could invite people over to our פֶּסַח סֵדֶר! This is not what YOU told us to do! You said that when we offer the קָרְבָּן it should be a "private occasion" or a *group* affair, but now we cannot do what You want!" This way, we are really asking 'ה to bring מָשִׁיחַ and rebuild the בֵּית הַמִּקְדָּשׁ immediately!
כָּל דְצָרִיךְ...		"*Whoever is in need.. let him come and eat...*" Here too we have the same question, "Who will hear us"? In this sentence we stress that we love opening our houses *all year long*, and helping whoever need our help in any manner. We ask 'ה that through this we should merit the final גְאוּלָה with the coming of מָשִׁיחַ right away.
יֵיתֵי וְיִפְסַח		"*Should come and celebrate the* פֶּסַח." The word יִפְסַח really means to bring the קָרְבָּן פֶּסַח. Here, however, it refers to the אֲפִיקוֹמָן, which we have today, instead of the קָרְבָּן.
הָשַׁתָּא...		"*This year* we are here, the next year in the land of Israel, This year we are slaves, the next year we should be free." Why do we say "this year" twice? This is teaching us that one might be in אֶרֶץ יִשְׂרָאֵל, and still *not* be free... The only true free person, is the one who is involved in the study of תוֹרָה. Here we ask that we should be in אֶרֶץ יִשְׂרָאֵל, *and* we should be *truly* free – studying the תוֹרָה. Also, even if for some sad reason we are not yet in אֶרֶץ יִשְׂרָאֵל, we still want to be "spiritually free" by being involved in the תוֹרָה and מִצְוֹת.
		And now.. our favorite part... when we hear your sweet voices ask...

FOUR QUESTIONS – מַה נִשְׁתַּנָה THE

And (when) it will be (that) your son will ask you later on (tomorrow) saying:	וְהָיָה כִּי יִשְׁאָלְךָ בִנְךָ מָחָר לֵאמֹר
"What is this?" (why are we celebrating?)	מַה זֹּאת
and you shall say to him	וְאָמַרְתָּ אֵלָיו
with a strong arm HaShem took us out of מִצְרַיִם, from the house of slavery (Shmos 13:14)	בְּחֹזֶק יָד הוֹצִיאָנוּ ה' מִמִּצְרַיִם מִבֵּית עֲבָדִים (שמות יג:יד)

מַה נִשְׁתַּנָה

We pour the second cup of wine and the children ask...

"Why is it different" – The Four Questions.

When talking about פֶּסַח in the תּוֹרָה, it says "כִּי יִשְׁאָלְךָ בִנְךָ... – *When your child will ask you*" and "וְהִגַּדְתָּ לְבִנְךָ. – *you should tell* your child..." We learn from this that the "telling" of the story of יְצִיאַת מִצְרַיִם on this night, must be in a way of *question and answer*. The child must first ask, only then does the father answer. This is why the "Four Questions" are so important.

This also teaches us, that parents should train their children to ask questions. This will ensure that the Jewish tradition will continue – through our children.

The first day of פֶּסַח, our יוֹם טוֹב of "education" and ט' בְּאָב – the day the בֵּית הַמִּקְדָּשׁ was destroyed, both fall on the *same day* of the week, every year . This shows a strong connection between the two days. If the children are educated the way they should be, we have פֶּסַח – redemption. Our חֲכָמִים say that the בֵּית הַמִּקְדָּשׁ was destroyed because the children were not properly educated.

If there are children at the סֵדֶר table, then the children usually ask, in order of age, from youngest to oldest. After the children ask the four questions, the adults ask them. If there are no children, then the adults ask the questions.

THE FOUR QUESTIONS - מַה נִשְׁתַּנָה

(In Hebrew, Yiddish and English[16])

Father I would like to ask you four questions:

טאַטע אִיךְ וועל בַּיי דִיר פְרֶעגֶן פִיר קַשְׁיוֹת

מַה נִשְׁתַּנָּה הַלַּיְלָה הַזֶּה מִכָּל הַלֵּילוֹת

Why is this night different from all other nights?

וואָס אִיז אַנְדֶערשׁ דִי נֶאַכְט פוּן פֶּסַח
פוּן אַלֶע נֶעכְט פוּן אַ גאַנְץ יאָר?

The first question is:

דִי עֶרְשְׁטֶע קַשְׁיָא אִיז:

❶ שֶׁבְּכָל הַלֵּילוֹת אָנוּ אוֹכְלִין חָמֵץ וּמַצָּה, הַלַּיְלָה הַזֶּה כֻּלּוֹ מַצָּה

On all other nights we may eat Chametz and
Matzah, and on this night only Matzah.

אַלֶע נֶעכְט פוּן אַ גאַנְץ יאָר
עֶסְן מִיר חָמֵץ אָדֶער מַצָּה,
אַבֶּער דִי נֶאַכְט פוּן פֶּסַח עֶסְן מִיר נאָר מַצָּה

The second question is:

דִי צְוֵוייטֶע קַשְׁיָא אִיז:

❷ שֶׁבְּכָל הַלֵּילוֹת אָנוּ אוֹכְלִין שְׁאָר יְרָקוֹת, הַלַּיְלָה הַזֶּה (כֻּלּוֹ) מָרוֹר

On all other nights we eat all kinds of
vegetables, and on this night, bitter ones.

אַלֶע נֶעכְט פוּן אַ גאַנְץ יאָר
עֶסְן מִיר אַלֶע עֶרְלֵיי גְרִינְסְן,
אַבֶּער דִי נֶאַכְט פוּן פֶּסַח
עֶסְן מִיר מָרוֹר - בִּיטֶערֶע גְרִינְסְן

The third question is:

דִי דְרִיטֶע קַשְׁיָא אִיז

❸ שֶׁבְּכָל הַלֵּילוֹת אֵין אָנוּ מַטְבִּילִין, אֲפִלוּ פַּעַם אֶחָת, הַלַּיְלָה הַזֶּה שְׁתֵּי פְעָמִים

On all other nights we are not required to
dip our vegetables even once, and on this
night we are required to do so twice.
(Once - כַּרְפַּס in salt water,
and the second time מָרוֹר in חֲרוֹסֶת)

אַלֶע נֶעכְט פוּן אַ גאַנְץ יאָר
טוּנְקֶען מִיר נִישְׁט אַיין אַפִילוּ אַיין מאָל,
אַבֶּער דִי נֶאַכְט פוּן פֶּסַח
טוּנְקֶען מִיר אַיין צְוֵוייַ מאָל,
אַיין מאָל כַּרְפַּס אִין זאַלְץ וואַסֶער,
דִי צְוֵוייטֶע מאָל מָרוֹר אִין חֲרוֹסֶת.

The fourth question is:

דִי פֶערְטֶע קַשְׁיָא אִיז:

❹ שֶׁבְּכָל הַלֵּילוֹת אָנוּ אוֹכְלִין בֵּין יוֹשְׁבִין וּבֵין מְסֻבִּין, הַלַּיְלָה הַזֶּה כֻּלָנוּ מְסֻבִּין

On all other nights we eat sitting upright
or reclining, and on this night we all recline.

אַלֶע נֶעכְט פוּן אַ גאַנְץ יאָר
עֶסְן מִיר סַיי זִיצֶנְדִיקֶערְהֵייט
אוּן סַיי אָנְגֶעלֶענְטֶערְהֵייט,
אַבֶּער דִי נֶאַכְט פוּן פֶּסַח
עֶסְן מִיר אַלֶע אָנְגֶעלֶענְטֶערְהֵייט

Father, I've asked you four questions,
now, please answer me.

טאַטע אִיךְ האָב בַּיי דִיר גֶעפְרֶעגְט פִיר קַשְׁיוֹת
יֶעצְט בִּיטֶע גִיב מִיר אַ תִּירוּץ

---

[16] In some הַגָּדוֹת the order of the questions is: מַטְבִּילִין – מַצָּה – מָרוֹר - מְסוּבִּין
© Rabbi C.B. Alevsky 5767/2007

continued...

As we see, the questions are about the מַצָּה, מָרוֹר, dipping and reclining.

Why are specifically these four questions "THE" four questions? There are many other interesting and even strange things we do on פֶּסַח night.

One answer is, because in these four questions, we have two מִצְווֹת מִדְרַבָּנָן (- commandments from the Rabbis) and two מִצְווֹת מִדְאוֹרַיְיתָא (- commandments from the תּוֹרָה). By putting them "together", it shows that both kinds of מִצְווֹת are equal in their importance.

The *Abarbanel* explains that these questions were chosen to show that in the סֵדֶר we "re-live" two opposite feelings, slavery and redemption. The מָרוֹר and dipping symbolize slavery, and the מַצָּה and reclining symbolize redemption.

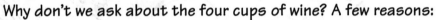

Why don't we ask about the four cups of wine? A few reasons:

❖ We don't drink all the four cups at once, and until now - at this part of the Seder when we ask the מַה נִּשְׁתַּנָּה - we only had one cup of wine just as we do on every שַׁבָּת and יוֹם טוֹב. So nothing "new" or "strange" happened yet regarding the wine... Even though we already poured the second cup, we are "used to" seeing wine on our tables on festive occasions.

❖ The מהר"ל says that the Four Questions are only about things that are directly connected to the main מִצְווֹת of the סֵדֶר, which are מַצָּה and מָרוֹר. The reclining is connected to the eating of the מַצָּה, and the dipping, to the מָרוֹר.

Then the father replies – in answer to the 4 questions:
(and we all say together)...

עֲבָדִים הָיִינוּ לְפַרְעֹה בְּמִצְרַיִם

"*We were enslaved to Pharaoh in Egypt...*, and 'ה freed us with awesome wonders and miracles." Therefore we tell the story at length.

וַיּוֹצִיאֵנוּ ה' אֱ-לֹקֵינוּ מִשָּׁם בְּיָד חֲזָקָה וּבִזְרֹעַ נְטוּיָה

"And Hashem our G-d took us out from there with a strong hand and outstretched arm (- with great miracles)."

בס"ד

פֶּסַח

continued...

וְאִלּוּ לֹא... **"If 'ה had not brought us out, we would still be slaves..."**

This means that even if we would have left מִצְרַיִם on our own - without 'ה's wonders and miracles, we would still be slaves. For example, if we would have waged war with them, won the war and left מִצְרַיִם on our own, then we would think that WE won the war, not 'ה, and there is no reason to thank Him. That is a slavery to a wrong idea!

מַעֲשֶׂה... **"It once happened..."**

This paragraph tells us that even our greatest sages – who definitely knew the story pretty well... would still tell the story of יְצִיאַת מִצְרַיִם at length.

אָמַר רַבִּי... **"Rabbi Elazar..."**

This paragraph shows the obligation to retell the story of יְצִיאַת מִצְרַיִם at all times.

בָּרוּךְ... **"Praised..." (Blessed is...)**

Here we see how every type of child is to be educated at the Seder. The famous "Four Sons" the Wise, Wicked, Simple and the One Who Does Not Know How To Ask, are discussed in this section. The הַגָּדָה tells us what each of them asks, and how they should be answered. We see their nature by the way they ask their questions.

NOTE: The תּוֹרָה it does not mention 4 sons as if they are all together asking questions... When it mentions the מִצְוָה for parents to tell the story of יְצִיאַת מִצְרַיִם in the תּוֹרָה, there are 4 different "styles" or approaches. From here we understand that 'ה is hinting to 4 different kinds of people that need to be told the story.

The Four Sons

הֶחָכָם — The Wise Son

מָה הָעֵדֹת וְהַחֻקִּים וְהַמִּשְׁפָּטִים אֲשֶׁר צִוָּה ה' אֱלֹקֵינוּ אֶתְכֶם - What are these laws... that 'ה our G-d commanded you.

The question of the חָכָם shows wisdom and interest in 'ה and His commandments to us.

He shows that he knows the difference between the three types of *Mitzvos*, the הָעֵדֹת, חֻקִים and מִשְׁפָּטִים, and asks about them.

The הַגָּדָה tells us to answer him by telling him all the laws of פֶּסַח, until the very last one – that we cannot eat after the אֲפִיקוֹמָן, which symbolizes the קָרְבַּן פֶּסַח.

This answer has a deeper message too. We tell the wise son that he should not "eat" anything after the אֲפִיקוֹמָן, this means that he should keep the "taste" of פֶּסַח – the "message" of פֶּסַח with him for the rest of the year. *(Moadim Uzmanim)*

Even though the חָכָם asks about the laws that 'ה commanded "you", he is not excluding himself from the laws – like the רָשָׁע. Some of the explanations of why he says "you" are:

❖ He is a קָטָן – under בַּר מִצְוָה and is asking about the קָרְבָּן which cannot be brought for a קָטָן.

❖ He is asking this question of his parents who were in מִצְרַיִם and experienced the יְצִיאַת מִצְרַיִם, while he himself was not there.

❖ The word "אֶתְכֶם – you" can be a combination of "אוֹתִי וְאֶתְכֶם – me and you." Meaning that the "you" he says – includes himself too.

רָשָׁע — The Wicked Son

מָה הָעֲבוֹדָה הַזֹּאת לָכֶם – "What does this service mean to you."

Here, the רָשָׁע *means* to exclude himself from the מִצְווֹת that 'ה gave us, and separates himself from the Jewish community.

The הַגָּדָה tells us to "blunt his teeth." This is an expression which means "answer him very sharply."

We tell him that the reason 'ה took us out was because we fulfilled His commandments then and continue to fulfill them now.

We say that "had he been there – in מִצְרַיִם – he would not have been saved." He would have either joined the Egyptians or died in מַכַּת חֹשֶׁךְ.

Sometimes, the only way to make an impression on a wicked person for him to do תְּשׁוּבָה, is to be very strict with him.

continued...

תָּם   מַה זֹּאת – "What is this?"

The simple son asks a simple question.

The   He wants to know the story of בְּנֵי יִשְׂרָאֵל in מִצְרַיִם and how we were taken out of our slavery.

Simple   We answer him by relating the story, and telling him that 'ה took us out with a strong arm.

Son   The simple son knows that we – the Jewish People – suffered many times throughout our history, and he might be losing hope about 'ה helping us out of this גָלוּת. Therefore, we mention that 'ה took us out of מִצְרַיִם with a "strong hand" – meaning that no job is too big for 'ה, and when He wants to He will take us out of our גָלוּת.

שֶׁאֵינוֹ יוֹדֵעַ לִשְׁאוֹל   This child is not yet mature enough to ask substantial (real) questions. We therefore tell him "For *this*... 'ה took us out." We show him the פֶּסַח, מַצָּה and מָרוֹר, and teach him about these מִצְווֹת. These are tangible (touchable) things that he can relate to better.

Does Not

Know To

Ask

Notice that the wise son sits next to the wicked one. The wise son knows that the תּוֹרָה and מִצְווֹת are the most important things in our lives and he feels bad for the wicked son/child that is wasting his/her life in nonsense! The חָכָם wants to teach the רָשָׁע the way of 'ה.

continued...

יָכוֹל...   "One might think..."

...explains when this special obligation (of telling the story) applies.

מִתְּחִלָה...   "In the beginning..."

...shows the deeper roots of the גָלוּת (exile), and our going out of מִצְרַיִם as the way to spiritual redemption.

וְהִיא שֶׁעָמְדָה   "And it is *this* that stood by us...."

The simple explanation is that "this" refers to what was just read in the previous paragraph in the הַגָּדָה. It talks about the בְּרִית – pact, that 'ה made with אַבְרָהָם that He will redeem us from גָלוּת – the Exile of his children to a strange land. So it is this promise that 'ה continues to keep whenever the Jews "get into trouble."

Another explanation:

"וְהִיא – *this*" – refers to our connection to the תּוֹרָה and 'ה.

In every generation there were (and are...) people that tried to harm and destroy us, and when we keep the תּוֹרָה, HaShem saves us from them.

Some say the גְּמַטְרִיָא (numerical value) of the letters of וְהִיא hint as follows:

ו	6	Sections of the מִשְׁנָה
ה	5	Books of the תּוֹרָה
י	10	Commandments
א	1	Hashem

meaning to say that it is this important "list" that keeps up surviving as a Nation.

צֵא וּלְמַד...   "Go out and learn..."

...the *Midrash* describes the details of the פֶּסַח story to its joyous end.

continued...

דָם וָאֵשׁ... | Here the הַגָּדָה, mentions the punishments that were inflicted on the מִצְרִים.

דָם צְפַרְדֵעַ... |

דְצַ"ךְ... | We name the punishments and the מַכּוֹת. Then we say the abbreviation words of the מַכּוֹת.

For each word we say, we pour some wine out of our cup, into a bowl.

There are different customs about how this wine is poured.

- Some dip their little finger into the cup and remove the wine with a "flick."

- Some pour the wine from the cup into a bowl that has a crack or "blemish."

The different customs about *how* the wine should be removed from the cup, can be connected to the different explanations of *why* we are saying these words:

Some explain that we are talking about how the "finger of 'ה" brought the punishments to the מִצְרִים, as it relates in the תּוֹרָה how the people of מִצְרִים claimed that the מַכּוֹת were "אֶצְבַּע אֱ-לֹקִים." According to this explanation, we dip our finger into the cup and remove the wine. *(Darkei Moshe)*

Others explain that the reason we pour the wine is, because of the פָּסוּק in מִשְׁלֵי that says: "Do not rejoice when your enemy falls." Therefore, while we mention the punishments that 'ה brought on the מִצְרִים, we still show our unhappiness that something 'ה created was punished, by spilling out something precious to us. *(Abarbanel)*

רַבִּי יְהוּדָה... | רַבִּי יְהוּדָה made signs for the 10 מַכּוֹת. The simple reason for this was to make it easier to remember all the מַכּוֹת in their correct order. (Remembering three words is easier than ten!)

דְצַ"ךְ עַדַ"שׁ בְּאַחַ"ב | Some say that these letters were engraved on מֹשֶׁה רַבֵּנוּ's staff.

דַּיֵּינוּ

"It would have been enough for us..."

In this famous song we praise 'ה for 15 different wonders and kindness He performed for us. In between each of them, we say "Had He only performed this one without the next one – דַּיֵּינוּ – it would have sufficed (been enough for) us.

רַבָּן גַּמְלִיאֵל...

The three main מִצְוֹת commanded for the סֵדֶר:

קָרְבַּן פֶּסַח   מַצָּה   מָרוֹר

רַבָּן גַּמְלִיאֵל says that in order to fulfill our obligation for the night, we need to talk about, explain and "do" these three מִצְוֹת.

Pesach:
Our Journey
to Freedom

MAGID: RUN FOR YOUR LIFE...

Magid isn't just the retelling of an event that happened to us thousands of years ago.

When we left Mitzrayim, we became a holy nation. This is the story of each one of us, happening over and over again. It is our constant, personal fight with our Yetzer Harah, our struggle to free ourselves from his clutches, to enable us to be who we are meant to be.

From Judah the Macabbee to Samson the Mighty to Houdini the Magician, Jews have always been trying to get freedom from something. It's in our blood to escape from where we are to move ever higher.

Leaving our personal Mitzrayim is like breathing to our Neshama.

When we talk about the Exodus, we are reminding ourselves why we came into this world, and what our job is here: to break through our own "chains", to grow spiritually and share the beauty of Hashem's Torah with the world.

רָחְצָה
Rachtzah

Washing

We wash our hands the way we do before eating bread. Three times on the right, then three times on the left. (Some wash 2 times on each hand.) We say the usual בְּרָכָה of עַל נְטִילַת יָדַיִם, and prepare to say...

בס"ד

Pesach's Journey to Freedom

ROCHTZA: <u>Do</u> something – wash your hands!

When Hashem took the us out of Egypt, he gave us more than freedom. He gave us the power to always free ourselves from the slavery of our Yetzer Harah, and become better people.

We have the power to go higher and become closer to Hashem. But every time we get closer to Hashem, we are reminded:

> We need to take that love and connection we feel towards Hashem
> and bring it down into an act of a Mitzvah.

Throughout the Seder, and throughout our lives as well, there is a constant cycle that brings us first close to Hashem, and then back to "the real world". We need to take the energy and strength we get from our special connection to Hashem, and put it into action: doing Mitzvot and learning Torah.

So after talking about the story of Mitzrayim, and focusing on how we can free our soul to unimagined heights, we stop and focus on the Mitzvah of washing our hands and prepare to make a blessing on bread. And not just any bread, but the Food of Faith: Matzah.

Matzah?! Hey – I haven't had that in a while – my mouth is watering!

מוֹצִיא
Motzie   Hamotzie

The customary בְּרָכָה over bread (in this case *Matzah*) ...
הַמוֹצִיא לֶחֶם מִן הָאָרֶץ.

We say this בְּרָכָה while we hold all three מַצוֹת in our hands.

Pesach: Our Journey to Freedom

MOTZIE: Food's Journey

Do you ever wonder why we enjoy our food so much? It's because we have a lot in common with food!

We and the bread share a common journey. The bread begins as a seed buried beneath the ground. And then, a miracle occurs: As it rots and loses its original form, it comes alive, and it sprouts and grows. As spring arrives, it pushes its way above the earth to find the sun, and then bears its fruits for the world.

We also began buried in Egypt, all but losing our identity as Jews. But that terrible place of slavery was like a fiery furnace that made us pure. Our birth as a nation came when we left Egypt in the month of spring.

So in this stop in our road trip, as you prepare to enjoy your matzah, think about how much work and effort goes into creating the flat, crispy and crunchy treat. Then think about how much Hashem has done for us to prepare us for our journey towards Freedom.

מַצָּה
Matzah

Matzah

We take the top מַצָּה together with the middle broken one, and make the special בְּרָכָה over the *Matzah* – עַל אֲכִילַת מַצָּה ... אֲשֶׁר קִדְּשָׁנוּ...

When we say the בְּרָכָה, we should have in mind the מַצָּה we will be eating later, including the מַצָּה of כּוֹרֵךְ, and the אֲפִיקוֹמָן.

We eat a כְּזַיִת (a measurement about the size of a *ripe* olive) from each מַצָּה.

We eat it reclining towards our left side (leaning on a pillow if possible) as a symbol of freedom.

Pesach:

Our Journey

to Freedom

MATZAH

Q: when do you get to actually EAT a Mitzvah?

A: Only on Pesach! Since the destruction of the Temple in Jerusalem, Matzah is the only opportunity we have to actually eat a mitzvah. That's right, the matzah you are eating is pure G-dliness. In fact, it has enough G-dly energy to blast your soul out of the deepest ditch into the highest heights.

The Zohar calls matzah "Bread of Emunah" and "Bread of Healing". Emunah means a lot more than just faith. Emunah is when you touch that place where your Neshamah and the essence of Hashem's light are one.

Eating matzah helps us plug into Hashem's essence, and gives our Neshama strength. We actually "feed" our Neshama when we eat Matzah!

How in the world, you may ask, can a mixture of water and wheat from the ground baked in an oven contain a spiritual cure?

Well, welcome to the world of the Jewish People, where there is no separation of body and soul, where objects become holy - like Tefillin, and our soul powers our emotions, mind and body. It's a place where bodies are healed by strengthening the soul and souls are nourished by the Mitzvot the body does of the body.

After all, we live in the world of a single Hashem, who made EVERYTHING, physical and spiritual alike.

So on this stop, we focus on doing things with our body - eat, sleep, laugh – to strengthen our Neshama and our connection to Hashem.

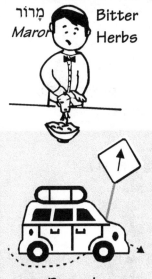

מָרוֹר
Maror
Bitter
Herbs

We take a כְּזַיִת of מָרוֹר, dip it into the חֲרוֹסֶת, and say

אֲשֶׁר קִדְּשָׁנוּ... עַל אֲכִילַת מָרוֹר.

We do *not* recline while we eat it.

Pesach:

Our Journey

to Freedom

MAROR: Bitterness that works!

So here we are, zooming along on the highway of life, and we've come to this POTHOLE. It's huge, it's dangerous, and lots of cars have lost their tires and even their wheels flying over this big crack in the ground. Let's take a minute and think about how many lives have been endangered because the Highway maintenance people haven't been doing their jobs. In fact, while I think about this I am getting angry, and even a little bitter.

What's good about bitterness? Why do we want to remember bad things, *the horror of our years of slavery and hardship?*

Actually, our bitterness in Egypt was and is the key to our redemption.

We never got used to Egypt. We never felt we belonged there.

We never said, "They are the masters and we are the slaves and that's the way it is." It always remained something we felt sad and angry about, something that was unjust and needed to change.

If it hadn't been that way, we probably would never have left. In fact, tradition tells us that 80% of the Jews said, "This is our land. How can we leave it?" And they stayed and died there.

But as for the rest of us, when Moses came and told us we were going to leave, we believed him. It was our bitterness that had preserved our faith.

But while we remember the sad times, and even cry about them, we need to know that we do not need to stay in that sad mood. We need to focus on what we can do to make sure things get better. Just like the sweet charoset we put on the bitter herbs, we need to direct the energy of our anger and bitterness towards making this world a better place.

Personally, we all have our own Egypt. You've got to know who you are and what your limitations are. But heaven forbid, don't make peace with them. The soul within you KNOWS NO LIMITS. Know you aren't perfect? Well, it's about time you realized that. But don't stop now. Get to work on yourself and make yourself better. You CAN do it!

So put on your yellow construction hat and FIX THAT POTHOLE. And tell everyone else to slow down as they drive by, because you are a Man (or Woman) at Work, fixing up the road of life!

כּוֹרֵךְ
Korech Sandwich

The very first documented "Sandwich" in history...

We take another כְּזַיִת of מָרוֹר, romaine lettuce and horseradish, make a "sandwich" with the *third* מַצָּה, and say:

"כֵּן עָשָׂה הִלֵּל ...Thus did Hillel..."

Then we eat our sandwich, reclining to the left side.

Pesach:

Our Journey

to Freedom

KORECH: WE'RE ALL IN THIS TOGETHER!

Let's get into orbit for this part of our trip. Sometimes we need to be above the world to get the right angle on things, and Korach is a perfect opportunity to blast off into outer space.

How does earth look from outer space,? Well, I've never been there, but the pictures taken from space show our world glowing in beautiful greens, tans and blues.

We all know that when we zoom in on the detail, our world does not look like that. Streets can be dirty, not all people act nice, and in some places, we can't even find a tree. But we know that from the bigger picture, the world is by far the best planet to live on... simply because there is no other place for us to live!

When we are living our life down below in this world, we see things like people fighting, or caring about things that aren't important like fancy cars, clothes or the latest Play Station or purse. Sometimes we see our Mitzvot as a bunch of do's and don'ts, and life is tough, full of responsibility and problems.

But from up high in Korach orbit, things look different.

We can see that all the Mitzvot are different expressions of a single spiritual path, all of us Jews are multiple faces to a single soul, and all the problems we encounter are testing our commitment to our journey.

Like separate instruments in a single orchestra, the world creates beautiful music in harmony under the leadership of the Greatest Conductor, Hashem.

Like astronauts blasting off into space, we need to think of everything we do and face in this world as part of our mission from Hashem. Taking out the garbage? Part of the job detail. Doing homework? That's preparing for our space walk.

When you start to think that way, then all the bitter, all the sweet and all the boring parts of life wrap together in a single tasty sandwich.

Preparing to land... Space Mission Accomplished!

שֻׁלְחָן עוֹרֵך
*Shulchan
Orech*

Meal time

Finally... we eat the festive יוֹם טוֹב meal...

Pesach:
Our Journey
to Freedom

SHULCHAN ORECH: Bring your food along!

After our Korach trip, we are ready to re-enter our atmosphere from our out-of-this-world experience.

We've escaped Egypt and reached a higher place inside ourselves. And now we start the process again – on a higher level. Because each time we reach higher, we turn around and bend down, and bring the parts of ourselves and our world that are not as holy up to our higher place. That's what freedom is: when you can turn around and free ALL the elements of your world and make them holy, not just your soul.

That's what we do when we eat every day - we take foods which grow from the earth, say a blessing over them and bring them into our journey as human beings. And when it's Shabbat or another Jewish holiday, we elevate them further and make them even holier. As for tonight, this meal is going to be truly Divine.

So those road stops for Matzah, Marror and Korach were just a taste for what's to come. Don't imagine we're just finally getting to sit down to a real meal now. We're reaching a higher state. And what a great way to do it!

Pass the chicken, please!

 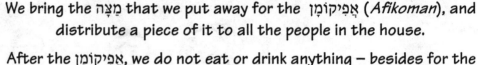
...ending with:

צָפוּן
Tzafun

The Afikoman

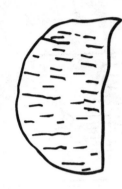

We bring the מַצָּה that we put away for the אֲפִיקוֹמָן (*Afikoman*), and distribute a piece of it to all the people in the house.

After the אֲפִיקוֹמָן, we do not eat or drink anything – besides for the 3rd and 4th cup of wine. So make sure you had your fill beforehand...

The word אֲפִיקוֹמָן, actually means "dessert." We eat the אֲפִיקוֹמָן reclining. On the first night, it must be eaten before midnight, just like the קָרְבַּן פֶּסַח had to be eaten before midnight.

Why do some "hide" the אֲפִיקוֹמָן?

The simple answer is that we do not want to eat it by mistake, earlier than we planned - so we put it away.

Another reason is similar to most of the strange things we do on this night: to arouse the curiosity of the children and keep them awake!

And then comes the "other" reason...

This is the story:

Since the אֲפִיקוֹמָן is what we eat in place of the קָרְבַּן פֶּסַח, it is a very important part of our celebration.

Now, knowing that the אֲפִיקוֹמָן is sooooo important, and Mother and Father cannot complete the סֵדֶר without it, some sneaky children devised a plan... A plan that will get them whatever they want... They hide the אֲפִיקוֹמָן from their parents and when it is time to eat it, they hold it ransom until they are promised what they want...

Some families do not follow this custom because, although the children "take" the אֲפִיקוֹמָן with their parents' knowledge, it is just a little too similar to stealing, and we should not get used to doing things that are "similar" to wrong things!

Pesach:

Our Journey

to Freedom

TZAFUN: THE INSIDE STORY...

We've been talking a lot about our soul. Do you know there is something even higher than our soul?

Deep inside our soul is a source of energy that we usually cannot reach, for good or bad. No matter what we do, we cannot really affect that inner power. The only way we can touch that part inside of us is when Hashem gives us the power to do it.

On Pesach night, we have that power. But only after all the steps are done before: Destroying our personal chametz, preparing our homes for freedom, the eleven steps of the Seder until now. When we have done all this work, and connected every part of ourselves to Hashem, that's when that power comes to us. Whether we feel it or not, tasteless as it may seem to have that dry cracker on a full stomach... the Matzah we eat now reaches deep into our core and transforms our very being.

We learn an important lesson from this stop on our journey:

Things you find to be inspiring or nice will take you forward in life. But to really make a real change, you need to do something that may go against our nature. You might find it embarrassing, or difficult, or even painful, but when you get past those barriers, you will get to a place where never imagined you could be. So don't let those roadblocks stop you. Find a way around them. Hashem has given you that power. Use it!

בֵּרַךְ *Berach* Bentching

We pour the third cup and say the בִּרְכַּת הַמָּזוֹן (*Bentching*), the blessing after a meal, over this cup.

Pesach:

Our Journey

to Freedom

BARECH: BRING ON THE BLESSINGS!

When we say Birchat Hamazon, we are showing that we trust in Hashem to provide for us always, and take care of our every need. Even if we don't know how He will do so, we know He will give us what we need.

When we say this out loud, with joy and sincerity, we actually start a powerful current that bounces back to us, giving us even more blessings than before. So the more we truly thank Hashem for things he has given us and will give us in the future, the more Hashem will give us.

Why did miracles happen in Egypt? Because we believed they would. Those who didn't believe in miracles, saw only plagues. To see a miracle, you need an open heart and mind, open enough to receive the blessings of Hashem.

That is the opening we make when we thank G-d for the miracle of our food.

We drink the third cup

We pour the cup for ...אֵלִיָּהוּ הַנָּבִיא

אֵלִיָּהוּ הַנָּבִיא comes to visit all Jewish homes on פֶּסַח night and "participates" in our סְדָרִים. We honor him with a cup of wine.

...שְׁפוֹךְ
Pour out..

We walk to the outside door with candles, open it and say: ...שְׁפוֹךְ, to show that we do not fear anything. In this זְכוּת, (merit) 'ה should bring מָשִׁיחַ and give the enemies of בְּנֵי יִשְׂרָאֵל what they deserve.

הַלֵּל Hallel   Praise

We continue to say parts of תְּהִלִּים (Psalms) which praise 'ה for what He has done for us. We also declare our faith in 'ה, - for the future.

The fourth cup is drunk here

Pesach:
Our Journey
to Freedom

HALLEL: MAKE THE LEAP

The ancient rabbis clued us in on a secret: Whatever Hashem tells us to do, He does Himself. Of course, there's a difference: We do it in our little human world. He does it on a very different level.

He told us to open our door on the night of Passover. So, tonight, He opens every door and every gateway to Heaven to every member of the Jewish People. To each one of us, regardless of what we have been doing in the past. Tonight is the chance to reach to the highest of spiritual levels.

There's nothing stopping you. Go leap for it! This is the Bungee Jump part of our Trip... Just that we are jumping UP!

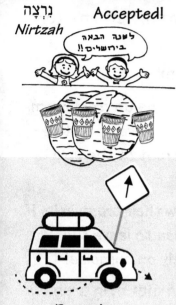

נִרְצָה
Nirtzah

Accepted!

לְשָׁנָה הַבָּאָה בִּירוּשָׁלַיִם!!

Pesach:

Our Journey

to Freedom

"Accepted" The Seder is completed with our prayers and service. These will surely be accepted by ה', and מָשִׁיחַ should come speedily!

Here come the famous words – and song...

לְשָׁנָה הַבָּאָה בִּירוּשָׁלָיִם

NIRTZAH: HASHEM, IT'S YOUR TURN!

Some people think we are meant to make a perfect world. But if that is what our Creator wanted, why did He make us such imperfect beings?

Rather, what He wants of us is our very humanness. Sometimes we do good. Sometimes we fall. But we keep on trying, and eventually we make some real changes in our lives and in the world around us.

And then, once we have done all we can - like our mothers helping us with our science fair project – Hashem makes sure to touch up the job and make it shine. (Does your mother really help you?! You're supposed to do it yourself!)

For over 3300 years we have been leaving Egypt. For over 3300 years we have been doing our human job of transforming the darkness of His world into light. And now it is His turn to lift us up, to banish the darkness forever, to make our work shine and... to leave the lights on so we can find our way back home.

And when that day will come, we'll have completed the longest road trip ever. Because we'll be have finally reached our final destination: Home in Yerushalayim, with Mashiach! May it happen now!

Doodle a Mashiach world or idea:

A BIT ABOUT THE תְּפִילוֹת

During all eight days of פֶּסַח we add the תְּפִילָה of יַעֲלֶה וְיָבוֹא in our תְּפִילַת הָעֲמִידָה – (or שְׁמוֹנָה עֶשְׂרֵה) and בִּרְכַת הַמָּזוֹן.

During the first two and last two days, we say the עֲמִידָה for the שָׁלֹשׁ רְגָלִים.

The first night of פֶּסַח is called "לֵיל שִׁימוּרִים" – the night that ה' guards us from harm. On this night for the קְרִיאַת שְׁמַע שֶׁעַל הַמִּטָה – the Shema we say before we go to bed - we say only the fist portion of שְׁמַע and וְאָהַבְתָּ, we do not say the rest of the שְׁמַע and all the תְּפִילוֹת - prayers afterwards.

Some have the custom to leave the house doors unlocked to show their trust in ה'. If the neighborhood is known as an unsafe one... it is not a good idea to leave the doors unlocked – because even when we do מִצְווֹת we are not to rely on miracles!

Starting מַשִּׁיב הָרוּחַ וּמוֹרִיד הַגֶּשֶׁם on the first day of פֶּסַח, in תְּפִילַת מוּסָף we do not say anymore in our עֲמִידָה. There are different customs regarding what replaces that phrase. Some say מוֹרִיד הַטָל, and some do not say anything in the place of מַשִּׁיב הָרוּחַ וּמוֹרִיד הַגֶּשֶׁם.

On שַׁבָּת-חוֹל הַמוֹעֵד some have the custom to say שִׁיר הַשִּׁירִים.

CHOL HAMOED - חֹל הַמּוֹעֵד

The first two days of פֶּסַח, are days of יוֹם טוֹב and are אֲסוּרִים בִּמְלָאכָה as we learned earlier. The next four days are חֹל הַמּוֹעֵד - the weekdays of the holiday.

Date	Day	We Celebrate	We...
טו נִיסָן	1	1st day of יוֹם טוֹב	Celebrate 1st סֵדֶר
טז נִיסָן	2	2nd day of יוֹם טוֹב	Celebrate 2nd סֵדֶר
יז נִיסָן	3	1st day of חֹל הַמּוֹעֵד	Family time!
חי נִיסָן	4	2nd day of חֹל הַמּוֹעֵד	Family time!
יט נִיסָן	5	3rd day of חֹל הַמּוֹעֵד	Family time!
כ נִיסָן	6	4th day of חֹל הַמּוֹעֵד	Family time!
כא נִיסָן	7	שְׁבִיעִי שֶׁל פֶּסַח	יוֹם טוֹב
כב נִיסָן	8	אַחֲרוֹן שֶׁל פֶּסַח	יוֹם טוֹב

During חֹל הַמּוֹעֵד, we are permitted to "work" or do מְלָאכוֹת on these conditions:

1. It is in preparation for food.

2. We would be losing money if we don't do it - like one's job.

Since preparing food involves many מְלָאכוֹת including the use of fire, we are allowed to do them all (and use fire) even when we are not preparing food.

On חֹל הַמּוֹעֵד:

We do not get haircuts, cut our nails[17] or write. If it is an urgent matter, like if one will lose money if they don't write, then writing is permitted.

We do not wash clothes unless it is necessary, like for a babies or children who dirty their clothes all too often.

There are different customs about putting on תְּפִילִין during חֹל הַמּוֹעֵד. Some do and some do not! One should usually follow his family or congregation's custom.

During חֹל הַמּוֹעֵד we add יַעֲלֶה וְיָבוֹא in our תְּפִילוֹת and say חֲצִי הַלֵּל - the "half" or "incomplete" הַלֵּל.

---

[17] If you know that your nails grow fast and you cut them right before יוֹם טוֹב intending to cut them again during Yom Tov – you may.

THE SEVENTH DAY OF PESACH – שְׁבִיעִי שֶׁל פֶּסַח

And the first day shall be a sacred (holy) Holiday and the seventh shall be a sacred Holiday for you.	וּבַיּוֹם הָרִאשׁוֹן מִקְרָא קֹדֶשׁ וּבַיּוֹם הַשְּׁבִיעִי מִקְרָא קֹדֶשׁ יִהְיֶה לָכֶם
No work shall be done in them (those days)	כָּל מְלָאכָה לֹא יֵעָשֶׂה בָהֶם
The only work that you may do, is that which is needed so that everyone will be able to eat. (Shemot 12:16)	אַךְ אֲשֶׁר יֵאָכֵל לְכָל נֶפֶשׁ הוּא לְבַדּוֹ יֵעָשֶׂה לָכֶם (שמות יב:טז)

The seventh day of פֶּסַח is the end of [18] פֶּסַח. Therefore we do not say the בְּרָכָה of שֶׁהֶחֱיָינוּ when we make קִידוּשׁ or light the יוֹם טוֹב candles.

On this day we commemorate the greatest miracle of all time: The splitting of the Red Sea – קְרִיעַת יַם סוּף

Some have the custom to remain awake during the night before שְׁבִיעִי שֶׁל פֶּסַח, studying תּוֹרָה and celebrating the great miracle ה' made for us.

Many communities (especially in Israel) have the custom to "re-create" the קְרִיעַת יַם סוּף is Shul... They pour water on the (non carpeted) floor of the Shul and dance through it until the water dries! What fun! (This should only be done with adult permission and supervision!)

Interestingly, when the Torah refers to the miracle of קְרִיעַת יַם סוּף, it does not mention the date in which the miracle happened. This is because although we were saved with such great wonders and miracles – the Egyptians however, were not having such fun drowning... and ה' is not happy when anyone of His creations suffer, even sinners. To show His disappointment about their suffering, Hashem did not place the date of this נֵס in the תּוֹרָה.

---

[18] It is **not a separate** יוֹם טוֹב – like שְׁמִינִי עֲצֶרֶת, the last day of סוּכּוֹת is.

Since 'ה is not happy, we too do not celebrate this יוֹם טוֹב to mark the downfall of our enemies. Rather, we celebrate that 'ה saved us. Interestingly, בְּנֵי יִשְׂרָאֵל were actually commanded to celebrate שְׁבִיעִי שֶׁל פֶּסַח even <u>before</u> קְרִיעַת יַם סוּף happened!

So what do we celebrate on this day? We celebrate the miracles that 'ה performed to save us. We remember the שִׁירַת הַיָּם – the song that מֹשֶׁה and בְּנֵי יִשְׂרָאֵל sang on this day. This is the אָז יָשִׁיר מֹשֶׁה we say every day in our תְּפִילַת שַׁחֲרִית.

THE LAST DAY OF PESACH – אַחֲרוֹן שֶׁל פֶּסַח

This is the last day of פֶּסַח. It is the יוֹם טוֹב שֵׁנִי שֶׁל גָּלוּיוֹת [19] - of the seventh day – שְׁבִיעִי שֶׁל פֶּסַח.

This day is a "repeat" of שְׁבִיעִי שֶׁל פֶּסַח with a few differences[20].

In חוּץ לָאָרֶץ (– outside of אֶרֶץ יִשְׂרָאֵל) the תְּפִילָה of יִזְכּוֹר – Remembrance, is said after the Torah reading. This is a תְּפִילָה in which people remember their parents and family who passed away. All those who have both parents alive (ב"ה) – leave the Shul during יִזְכּוֹר.

Some of those who during פֶּסַח keep away from eating מַצָּה שְׁרוּיָ'ה - Matzah that has been soaked in a liquid - on this Eighth Day however, they do eat מַצָּה שְׁרוּיָ'ה. They get to eat Matzah balls and Matzah brie! Now that's something to look forward too!

On מוֹצָאֵי יוֹם טוֹב – it is VERY IMPORTANT to wait about an hour before we start eating our חָמֵץ or even using the חָמֵץ utensils that we sold to the non Jew. This hour gives the rabbi enough time to "buy back" your Chametz from the person to whom he sold it.

The day following the יוֹם טוֹב is known as אִסְרוּ חַג - and it is forbidden to fast on this day.

---

19 (This is explained in the footnote on page 10)

20 Those who follow the Baal Shem Tov's custom, end פֶּסַח with "סְעוּדַת מָשִׁיחַ"—a festive meal complete with Matzah and four cups of wine during which they celebrate the coming of מָשִׁיחַ. The feast begins before sunset and continues until after nightfall. Nightfall is the official end of Passover

סְפִירַת הָעוֹמֶר – COUNTING THE OMER

...and you will reap (cut off) its harvest	...וּקְצַרְתֶּם אֶת קְצִירָהּ
you must bring an Omer of the first reaping to the Cohen	וַהֲבֵאתֶם אֶת עֹמֶר רֵאשִׁית קְצִירְכֶם אֶל הַכֹּהֵן
after the first day of the Holiday (Pesach) the Cohen shall make this wave-offering.	...מִמָּחֳרַת הַשַּׁבָּת יְנִיפֶנּוּ הַכֹּהֵן (בְּמִדְבָּר כג,ט)
You shall count for yourselves seven complete weeks, after the first day of the Holiday (Pesach)	וּסְפַרְתֶּם לָכֶם מִמָּחֳרַת הַשַּׁבָּת
from the day you brought the Omer as a wave-offering	מִיּוֹם הֲבִיאֲכֶם אֶת עֹמֶר הַתְּנוּפָה
They shall be seven complete weeks...	שֶׁבַע שַׁבָּתוֹת, תְּמִימֹת תִּהְיֶינָה
Until the day after the seven weeks you shall count (- when there will be a total of) fifty days	עַד מִמָּחֳרַת הַשַּׁבָּת הַשְּׁבִיעִת תִּסְפְּרוּ חֲמִשִּׁים יוֹם
And you shall present a new meal-offering to Hashem (Bamidbar 23:15-16)	וְהִקְרַבְתֶּם מִנְחָה חֲדָשָׁה לַה' (בְּמִדְבָּר כג:טו-ז)

The תּוֹרָה tells us that on the 2nd day of פֶּסַח, we should bring a קָרְבָּן - offering of barley, in the amount of one עוֹמֶר - Omer. The Omer is a name of a certain measurement.

People were only allowed to eat from the new produce of their fields after the עוֹמֶר קָרְבָּן was brought.

From the 2nd day of פֶּסַח, we have the מִצְוָה to COUNT SEVEN COMPLETE WEEKS – forty nine days.

The תּוֹרָה tells us that the 50th day is a יוֹם טוֹב called עֲצֶרֶת – "stopping". It is a מִקְרָא קוֹדֶשׁ – a holy day of gathering, that is אָסוּר בִּמְלָאכָה. On this day we offer a special קָרְבָּן - from the newly harvested wheat.

This 50th day is our יוֹם טוֹב of שָׁבוּעוֹת.

This counting, from the 2nd day of פֶּסַח until (and including) the day before שָׁבוּעוֹת is called: סְפִירַת הָעוֹמֶר.

סְפִירַת הָעוֹמֶר Some laws of

1. We count the סְפִירָה every day – for 49 days.

2. We count at night, after the stars come out.

3. Since it is a מִצְוָה – commandment - we make the בְּרָכָה:

בָּא״י אֱמֶ״הָ אקב״וְן עַל סְפִירַת הָעוֹמֶר

4. We recite the בְּרָכָה standing.

5. We start from the 2nd night of פֶּסַח – after תְּפִילַת עַרְבִית - before the 2nd סֵדֶר - פֶּסַח.[21]

6. Each night we count for the NEXT calendar day, since our "days" begin at night.

For example: If Monday is the 2nd day of the עוֹמֶר, Tuesday is the 3rd day, and Wednesday is the 4th day, then, on *Monday night* we count "שְׁלֹשָׁה יָמִים לָעוֹמֶר three days of the Omer", for Tuesday, and on *Tuesday night*, we count "אַרְבָּעָה יָמִים לָעוֹמֶר - four days of the Omer" for Wednesday etc.

7. We make the בְּרָכָה only when we count the סְפִירָה in the proper time, at night.

If one missed counting the סְפִירָה at night, s/he still counts the next day *without* the בְּרָכָה.

The next night s/he counts again *with* the בְּרָכָה.

If - after missing one night's count - one missed counting again that next day, s/he continues counting the סְפִירָה for the rest of the days *without* the בְּרָכָה.

8. Since this is a מִצְוָה שֶׁהַזְּמַן גְרָמָא[22] – woman are not obligated to fulfill this מִצְוָה, but they still make the בְּרָכָה when they fulfill the מִצְוָה.

At the end of this book there are 3 סְפִירָה charts. They is a "custom made" for the years 2007 and 2008 as noted on the top of the chart, and a blank one. If you are using this book in a different year, please check your Jewish Calendar to find the

---

[21] Some count the 1st סְפִירָה during the סֵדֶר

[22] This is a מִצְוָה that is connected to a specific time – and women are not *obligated* to fulfill מִצְוֹת שֶׁהַזְּמַן גְרָמָא.

correct counting days and fill in your blank chart accordingly. All you need to do is fill in the days of the week in their proper place.

PLEASE MAKE SURE TO USE THIS YEAR'S CHART!

Please cut out the chart for this year and have your teacher or parent LAMINATE it. Then you can post it on your fridge or on your desk, or another noticeable place and use it as your personal reminder for counting the סְפִירָה! If it is laminated – you can use an Erasable Marker or cute stickers to mark off the dates you've already counted the סְפִירָה.

Please ask your teacher or parent to make many copies of the Sefirah chart, and share them with your family and friends! This way you are helping others do a מִצְוָה!

That's all for now!

I enjoyed putting this book together – I hope enjoyed it too!

I would love to hear your corrections comments and suggestions on this book.

What you liked and what you didn't…

What you want to see more of – and what you want to see less of.

If you have an idea you think would fit well in this book please suggest it!

It may get in next printing!

Please email your comments to ToolsforTorah@Gmail.com

Visit www.ToolsForTorah.com for more fun Tools for Torah!

Next we have some Pesach songs! – Enjoy!

After that are your Sefirah Chart, then comes the workbook! Good Luck!

All the best!

Rabbi Chaim B. Alevsky

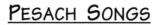

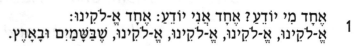

PESACH SONGS
YOU CAN HEAR MOST OF THESE SONGS ON THE
"PESACH'S GREATEST HITS" CD!
AVAILABLE AT BOOKS STORES OR ONLINE AT
WWW.TOOLSFORTORAH.COM

1 אֶחָד מִי יוֹדֵעַ? אֶחָד אֲנִי יוֹדֵעַ: אֶחָד אֱ-לֹקֵינוּ:
אֱ-לֹקֵינוּ, אֱ-לֹקֵינוּ, אֱ-לֹקֵינוּ, שֶׁבַּשָּׁמַיִם וּבָאָרֶץ.

2 שְׁנַיִם מִי יוֹדֵעַ? שְׁנַיִם אֲנִי יוֹדֵעַ: שְׁנֵי לֻחוֹת הַבְּרִית, אֶחָד אֱ-לֹקֵינוּ:
אֱ-לֹקֵינוּ, אֱ-לֹקֵינוּ, אֱ-לֹקֵינוּ, שֶׁבַּשָּׁמַיִם וּבָאָרֶץ.

3 שְׁלֹשָׁה מִי יוֹדֵעַ? שְׁלֹשָׁה אֲנִי יוֹדֵעַ: שְׁלֹשָׁה אָבוֹת, שְׁנֵי לֻחוֹת הַבְּרִית, אֶחָד אֱ-לֹקֵינוּ:
אֱ-לֹקֵינוּ, אֱ-לֹקֵינוּ, אֱ-לֹקֵינוּ, שֶׁבַּשָּׁמַיִם וּבָאָרֶץ.

4 אַרְבַּע מִי יוֹדֵעַ? אַרְבַּע אֲנִי יוֹדֵעַ: אַרְבַּע אִמָּהוֹת, שְׁלֹשָׁה אָבוֹת, שְׁנֵי לֻחוֹת הַבְּרִית, אֶחָד אֱ-לֹקֵינוּ... שֶׁבַּשָּׁמַיִם וּבָאָרֶץ.

5 חֲמִשָּׁה מִי יוֹדֵעַ? חֲמִשָּׁה אֲנִי יוֹדֵעַ: חֲמִשָּׁה חוּמְשֵׁי תוֹרָה, אַרְבַּע אִמָּהוֹת, שְׁלֹשָׁה אָבוֹת, שְׁנֵי לֻחוֹת הַבְּרִית, אֶחָד אֱ-לֹקֵינוּ... שֶׁבַּשָּׁמַיִם וּבָאָרֶץ.

6 שִׁשָּׁה מִי יוֹדֵעַ? שִׁשָּׁה אֲנִי יוֹדֵעַ: שִׁשָּׁה סִדְרֵי מִשְׁנָה, חֲמִשָּׁה חוּמְשֵׁי תוֹרָה, אַרְבַּע אִמָּהוֹת, שְׁלֹשָׁה אָבוֹת, שְׁנֵי לֻחוֹת הַבְּרִית, אֶחָד אֱ-לֹקֵינוּ... שֶׁבַּשָּׁמַיִם וּבָאָרֶץ.

7 שִׁבְעָה מִי יוֹדֵעַ? שִׁבְעָה אֲנִי יוֹדֵעַ: שִׁבְעָה יְמֵי שַׁבַּתָּא, שִׁשָּׁה סִדְרֵי מִשְׁנָה, חֲמִשָּׁה חוּמְשֵׁי תוֹרָה, אַרְבַּע אִמָּהוֹת, שְׁלֹשָׁה אָבוֹת, שְׁנֵי לֻחוֹת הַבְּרִית, אֶחָד אֱ-לֹקֵינוּ... שֶׁבַּשָּׁמַיִם וּבָאָרֶץ.

8 שְׁמוֹנָה מִי יוֹדֵעַ? שְׁמוֹנָה אֲנִי יוֹדֵעַ: שְׁמוֹנָה יְמֵי מִילָה, שִׁבְעָה יְמֵי שַׁבַּתָּא, שִׁשָּׁה סִדְרֵי מִשְׁנָה, חֲמִשָּׁה חוּמְשֵׁי תוֹרָה, אַרְבַּע אִמָּהוֹת, שְׁלֹשָׁה אָבוֹת, שְׁנֵי לֻחוֹת הַבְּרִית, אֶחָד אֱ-לֹקֵינוּ... שֶׁבַּשָּׁמַיִם וּבָאָרֶץ.

9 תִּשְׁעָה מִי יוֹדֵעַ? תִּשְׁעָה אֲנִי יוֹדֵעַ: תִּשְׁעָה יַרְחֵי לֵדָה, שְׁמוֹנָה יְמֵי מִילָה, שִׁבְעָה יְמֵי שַׁבַּתָּא, שִׁשָּׁה סִדְרֵי מִשְׁנָה, חֲמִשָּׁה חוּמְשֵׁי תוֹרָה, אַרְבַּע אִמָּהוֹת, שְׁלֹשָׁה אָבוֹת, שְׁנֵי לֻחוֹת הַבְּרִית, אֶחָד אֱ-לֹקֵינוּ... שֶׁבַּשָּׁמַיִם וּבָאָרֶץ.

10 עֲשָׂרָה מִי יוֹדֵעַ? עֲשָׂרָה אֲנִי יוֹדֵעַ: עֲשָׂרָה דִּבְּרַיָּא, תִּשְׁעָה יַרְחֵי לֵדָה, שְׁמוֹנָה יְמֵי מִילָה, שִׁבְעָה יְמֵי שַׁבַּתָּא, שִׁשָּׁה סִדְרֵי מִשְׁנָה, חֲמִשָּׁה חוּמְשֵׁי תוֹרָה, אַרְבַּע אִמָּהוֹת, שְׁלֹשָׁה אָבוֹת, שְׁנֵי לֻחוֹת הַבְּרִית, אֶחָד אֱ-לֹקֵינוּ... שֶׁבַּשָּׁמַיִם וּבָאָרֶץ.

11 אַחַד עָשָׂר מִי יוֹדֵעַ? אַחַד עָשָׂר אֲנִי יוֹדֵעַ: אַחַד עָשָׂר כּוֹכְבַיָּא, עֲשָׂרָה דִּבְּרַיָּא, תִּשְׁעָה יַרְחֵי לֵדָה, שְׁמוֹנָה יְמֵי מִילָה, שִׁבְעָה יְמֵי שַׁבַּתָּא, שִׁשָּׁה סִדְרֵי מִשְׁנָה, חֲמִשָּׁה חוּמְשֵׁי תוֹרָה, אַרְבַּע אִמָּהוֹת, שְׁלֹשָׁה אָבוֹת, שְׁנֵי לֻחוֹת הַבְּרִית, אֶחָד אֱ-לֹקֵינוּ... שֶׁבַּשָּׁמַיִם וּבָאָרֶץ.

12 שְׁנֵים עָשָׂר מִי יוֹדֵעַ? שְׁנֵים עָשָׂר אֲנִי יוֹדֵעַ: שְׁנֵים עָשָׂר שִׁבְטַיָּא, אַחַד עָשָׂר כּוֹכְבַיָּא, עֲשָׂרָה דִּבְּרַיָּא, תִּשְׁעָה יַרְחֵי לֵדָה, שְׁמוֹנָה יְמֵי מִילָה, שִׁבְעָה יְמֵי שַׁבַּתָּא, שִׁשָּׁה סִדְרֵי מִשְׁנָה, חֲמִשָּׁה חוּמְשֵׁי תוֹרָה, אַרְבַּע אִמָּהוֹת, שְׁלֹשָׁה אָבוֹת, שְׁנֵי לֻחוֹת הַבְּרִית, אֶחָד אֱ-לֹקֵינוּ... שֶׁבַּשָּׁמַיִם וּבָאָרֶץ.

13 שְׁלֹשָׁה עָשָׂר מִי יוֹדֵעַ? שְׁלֹשָׁה עָשָׂר אֲנִי יוֹדֵעַ: שְׁלֹשָׁה עָשָׂר מִדַּיָּא, שְׁנֵים עָשָׂר שִׁבְטַיָּא, אַחַד עָשָׂר כּוֹכְבַיָּא, עֲשָׂרָה דִּבְּרַיָּא, תִּשְׁעָה יַרְחֵי לֵדָה, שְׁמוֹנָה יְמֵי מִילָה, שִׁבְעָה יְמֵי שַׁבַּתָּא, שִׁשָּׁה סִדְרֵי מִשְׁנָה, חֲמִשָּׁה חוּמְשֵׁי תוֹרָה, אַרְבַּע אִמָּהוֹת, שְׁלֹשָׁה אָבוֹת, שְׁנֵי לֻחוֹת הַבְּרִית, אֶחָד אֱ-לֹקֵינוּ... שֶׁבַּשָּׁמַיִם וּבָאָרֶץ.

WHO KNOWS ONE?

Who knows one?

I know one!

One is Hashem, one is Hashem, one is Hashem

In the heavens and the earth.

(*I said a ooh, ahh, oo-ah-ah* x2)

Who knows two?...

Two are the luchos that Moshe brought,

And one is Hashem...

Three are the fathers...

Four are the mothers...

Five are the books of the Torah...

Six are the books of the Mishna...

Seven are the days of the week...

Eight are the days before a bris mila...

Nine are the months before a baby's born...

Ten are the Aseres Hadibros / Ten Commandments ...

Eleven are the stars in Yosef's dream...

Twelve are the tribes of Yisrael...

Thirteen are the Midot of Hashem...

Fourteen are the books of the Rambam...

פֶּסַח

עַל אַחַת כַּמָּה וְכַמָּה טוֹבָה כְפוּלָה
וּמְכֻפֶּלֶת לַמָּקוֹם עָלֵינוּ .

הוֹצִיאָנוּ מִמִּצְרַיִם . עָשָׂה בָהֶם שְׁפָטִים .

עָשָׂה בֵאלֹהֵיהֶם . הָרַג בְּכוֹרֵיהֶם .

נָתַן לָנוּ אֶת מָמוֹנָם . קָרַע לָנוּ אֶת הַיָּם .

הֶעֱבִירָנוּ בְתוֹכוֹ בֶּחָרָבָה .

שִׁקַּע צָרֵינוּ בְּתוֹכוֹ .

סִפֵּק צָרְכֵּנוּ בַּמִּדְבָּר אַרְבָּעִים שָׁנָה .

הֶאֱכִילָנוּ אֶת הַמָּן .

נָתַן לָנוּ אֶת הַשַּׁבָּת . קֵרְבָנוּ לִפְנֵי הַר סִינַי .

נָתַן לָנוּ אֶת הַתּוֹרָה . הִכְנִיסָנוּ לְאֶרֶץ יִשְׂרָאֵל .

וּבָנָה לָנוּ אֶת בֵּית הַבְּחִירָה לְכַפֵּר עַל כָּל
עֲווֹנוֹתֵינוּ :

אִלּוּ הוֹצִיאָנוּ מִמִּצְרַיִם
וְלֹא עָשָׂה בָהֶם שְׁפָטִים   דַּיֵּנוּ :

אִלּוּ עָשָׂה בָהֶם שְׁפָטִים
וְלֹא עָשָׂה בֵאלֹהֵיהֶם   דַּיֵּנוּ :

אִלּוּ עָשָׂה בֵאלֹהֵיהֶם
וְלֹא הָרַג אֶת בְּכוֹרֵיהֶם   דַּיֵּנוּ :

אִלּוּ הָרַג אֶת בְּכוֹרֵיהֶם
וְלֹא נָתַן לָנוּ אֶת מָמוֹנָם   דַּיֵּנוּ :

אִלּוּ נָתַן לָנוּ אֶת מָמוֹנָם
וְלֹא קָרַע לָנוּ אֶת הַיָּם   דַּיֵּנוּ :

אִלּוּ קָרַע לָנוּ אֶת הַיָּם
וְלֹא הֶעֱבִירָנוּ בְתוֹכוֹ בֶּחָרָבָה   דַּיֵּנוּ :

אִלּוּ הֶעֱבִירָנוּ בְתוֹכוֹ בֶּחָרָבָה
וְלֹא שִׁקַּע צָרֵינוּ בְּתוֹכוֹ   דַּיֵּנוּ :

אִלּוּ שִׁקַּע צָרֵינוּ בְּתוֹכוֹ
וְלֹא סִפֵּק צָרְכֵּנוּ בַּמִּדְבָּר אַרְבָּעִים שָׁנָה   דַּיֵּנוּ :

אִלּוּ סִפֵּק צָרְכֵּנוּ בַּמִּדְבָּר אַרְבָּעִים שָׁנָה
וְלֹא הֶאֱכִילָנוּ אֶת הַמָּן   דַּיֵּנוּ :

אִלּוּ הֶאֱכִילָנוּ אֶת הַמָּן
וְלֹא נָתַן לָנוּ אֶת הַשַּׁבָּת   דַּיֵּנוּ :

אִלּוּ נָתַן לָנוּ אֶת הַשַּׁבָּת
וְלֹא קֵרְבָנוּ לִפְנֵי הַר סִינַי   דַּיֵּנוּ :

אִלּוּ קֵרְבָנוּ לִפְנֵי הַר סִינַי
וְלֹא נָתַן לָנוּ אֶת הַתּוֹרָה   דַּיֵּנוּ :

אִלּוּ נָתַן לָנוּ אֶת הַתּוֹרָה
וְלֹא הִכְנִיסָנוּ לְאֶרֶץ יִשְׂרָאֵל   דַּיֵּנוּ :

אִלּוּ הִכְנִיסָנוּ לְאֶרֶץ יִשְׂרָאֵל
וְלֹא בָּנָה לָנוּ אֶת בֵּית הַמִּקְדָּשׁ   דַּיֵּנוּ :

There was a little mouse, who lived in a house
She ate bread crumbs all day, all day

She found them in the closet,
she found them on the floor
And when she was hungry,
she found some more

But one fine morning she jumped to her feet
She looked here, she looked there, but there was
not one crumb to eat

Yes, you guessed, it was Pesach time,
And our little mouse found Matzah and wine

She ate and she drank, and I'm pleased to say
She thanked Hashem in her own little way

פֶּסַח

חַד גַּדְיָא

1   חַד גַּדְיָא, חַד גַּדְיָא: דְּזַבִּין אַבָּא בִּתְרֵי זוּזֵי, חַד גַּדְיָא, חַד גַּדְיָא.

2   וְאָתָא שׁוּנְרָא, וְאָכְלָה לְגַדְיָא, דְּזַבִּין אַבָּא בִּתְרֵי זוּזֵי, חַד גַּדְיָא, חַד גַּדְיָא.

3   וְאָתָא כַלְבָּא, וְנָשַׁךְ לְשׁוּנְרָא, דְּאָכְלָה לְגַדְיָא, דְּזַבִּין אַבָּא בִּתְרֵי זוּזֵי, חַד גַּדְיָא, חַד גַּדְיָא.

4   וְאָתָא חוּטְרָא, וְהִכָּה לְכַלְבָּא, דְּנָשַׁךְ לְשׁוּנְרָא, דְּאָכְלָה לְגַדְיָא, דְּזַבִּין אַבָּא בִּתְרֵי זוּזֵי, חַד גַּדְיָא, חַד גַּדְיָא.

5   וְאָתָא נוּרָא, וְשָׂרַף לְחוּטְרָא, דְּהִכָּה לְכַלְבָּא, דְּנָשַׁךְ לְשׁוּנְרָא, דְּאָכְלָה לְגַדְיָא, דְּזַבִּין אַבָּא בִּתְרֵי זוּזֵי, חַד גַּדְיָא, חַד גַּדְיָא.

6   וְאָתָא מַיָּא, וְכָבָה לְנוּרָא, דְּשָׂרַף לְחוּטְרָא, דְּהִכָּה לְכַלְבָּא, דְּנָשַׁךְ לְשׁוּנְרָא, דְּאָכְלָה לְגַדְיָא, דְּזַבִּין אַבָּא בִּתְרֵי זוּזֵי, חַד גַּדְיָא, חַד גַּדְיָא.

7   וְאָתָא תוֹרָא, וְשָׁתָא לְמַיָּא, דְּכָבָה לְנוּרָא, דְּשָׂרַף לְחוּטְרָא, דְּהִכָּה לְכַלְבָּא, דְּנָשַׁךְ לְשׁוּנְרָא, דְּאָכְלָה לְגַדְיָא, דְּזַבִּין אַבָּא בִּתְרֵי זוּזֵי, חַד גַּדְיָא, חַד גַּדְיָא.

8   וְאָתָא הַשּׁוֹחֵט, וְשָׁחַט לְתוֹרָא, דְּשָׁתָא לְמַיָּא, דְּכָבָה לְנוּרָא, דְּשָׂרַף לְחוּטְרָא, דְּהִכָּה לְכַלְבָּא, דְּנָשַׁךְ לְשׁוּנְרָא, דְּאָכְלָה לְגַדְיָא, דְּזַבִּין אַבָּא בִּתְרֵי זוּזֵי, חַד גַּדְיָא, חַד גַּדְיָא.

9   וְאָתָא מַלְאַךְ הַמָּוֶת, וְשָׁחַט לְשׁוֹחֵט, דְּשָׁחַט לְתוֹרָא, דְּשָׁתָא לְמַיָּא, דְּכָבָה לְנוּרָא, דְּשָׂרַף לְחוּטְרָא, דְּהִכָּה לְכַלְבָּא, דְּנָשַׁךְ לְשׁוּנְרָא, דְּאָכְלָה לְגַדְיָא, דְּזַבִּין אַבָּא בִּתְרֵי זוּזֵי, חַד גַּדְיָא, חַד גַּדְיָא.

10   וְאָתָא הַקָּדוֹשׁ בָּרוּךְ הוּא, וְשָׁחַט לְמַלְאַךְ הַמָּוֶת, דְּשָׁחַט לְשׁוֹחֵט, דְּשָׁחַט לְתוֹרָא, דְּשָׁתָא לְמַיָּא, דְּכָבָה לְנוּרָא, דְּשָׂרַף לְחוּטְרָא, דְּהִכָּה לְכַלְבָּא, דְּנָשַׁךְ לְשׁוּנְרָא, דְּאָכְלָה לְגַדְיָא, דְּזַבִּין אַבָּא בִּתְרֵי זוּזֵי, חַד גַּדְיָא, חַד גַּדְיָא.

---

1   עֲבָדִים הָיִינוּ לְפַרְעֹה בְּמִצְרַיִם – עַתָּה - בְּנֵי חוֹרִין

קַדֵּשׁ. וּרְחַץ. כַּרְפַּס. יַחַץ. מַגִּיד. רָחְצָה. מוֹצִיא מַצָּה.

2   מָרוֹר. כּוֹרֵךְ. שֻׁלְחָן עוֹרֵךְ. צָפוּן. בָּרֵךְ. הַלֵּל. נִרְצָה.

וְהִיא שֶׁעָמְדָה לַאֲבוֹתֵינוּ וְלָנוּ. שֶׁלֹּא אֶחָד בִּלְבָד, עָמַד עָלֵינוּ לְכַלּוֹתֵנוּ.

3   אֶלָּא שֶׁבְּכָל דּוֹר וָדוֹר, עוֹמְדִים עָלֵינוּ לְכַלּוֹתֵנוּ. וְהַקָּדוֹשׁ בָּרוּךְ הוּא מַצִּילֵנוּ מִיָּדָם

---

4   דָּם. צְפַרְדֵּעַ. כִּנִּים. עָרוֹב. דֶּבֶר. שְׁחִין. בָּרָד. אַרְבֶּה. חֹשֶׁךְ. מַכַּת בְּכוֹרוֹת.

---

5   אֵלִיָּהוּ הַנָּבִיא, אֵלִיָּהוּ הַתִּשְׁבִּי, אֵלִיָּהוּ הַגִּלְעָדִי בִּמְהֵרָה יָבוֹא אֵלֵינוּ עִם מָשִׁיחַ בֶּן דָּוִד

---

6   **לְשָׁנָה הַבָּאָה בִּירוּשָׁלָיִם!**

THE סִימָנֵי הַסֵּדֶר WITH THE COMMONLY KNOWN *YIDDISH* EXPLANATION

וֶוען דֶער טאַטֶע קוּמט אַהֵיים פוּן שׁוּל מאַכט עֶר בּאַלד קידוּשׁ, כְּדֵי דִי קִינדֶער זאָלֶן נִישׁט אַיינשׁלאָפֶן, אוּן זֵיי זאָלֶן פְרֶעגְן דִי מַה נִשְׁתַּנָה.	קַדֵּשׁ
מֶען וואַשׁט דִי הֶענט, אָבֶּער מֶען מאַכט נִישׁט קֵיין בְּרָכָה עַל נְטִילַת יָדָיִם.	וּרְחַץ
מֶען נֶעמט אַ שׁטִיקֶל צִיבֶּעלֶע אָדֶער אַ קאַרטאָפֶל, וֶוייניקֶער פוּן אַ כְּזַיִת, מֶען טוּנקט עֶס אַיין אִין זאַלץ וואַסֶער אוּן מֶען מאַכט אַ בְּרָכָה בּוֹרֵא פְּרִי הָאֲדָמָה. מֶען האַט אִין זִינֶען דִי בְּרָכָה זאָל פַטְרְ'ן אוֹיך דִי מָרוֹר. דִי כַּרְפַּס עֶסט מֶען נִישׁט אָנגֶעלֶענטֶערהֵייט.	כַּרְפַּס
מֶען צוּטֵיילט דִי מִיטֶעלְסטֶע מַצָה אוֹיף צְוֵוי חֲלָקִים, אֵיין חֵלֶק גְרֶעסֶער פוּן דֶעם צְוֵוייטֶן. דֶעם גְרֶעסֶערן חֵלֶק לֵייגְט מֶען אַוֶוועק פאַר אַפִיקוֹמָן, אוּן דֶעם קְלֵענֶערן לאָזט מֶען אִיבֶּער צְוִוישֶׁן דִי צְוֵוי מַצוֹת.	יַחַץ
מֶען זאָגט דִי הַגָּדָה אוּן דִי קִינדֶער פְרֶעגְן מַה נִשְׁתַּנָה.	מַגִּיד
מֶען וואַשׁט דִי הֶענט אוּן מֶען מאַכט יֶע אַ בְּרָכָה עַל נְטִילַת יָדָיִם.	רָחְצָה
מֶען נֶעמט דִי דְרַיי מַצוֹת אִין דֶער האַנט, אוּן מֶען מאַכט אַ בְּרָכָה הַמוֹצִיא לֶחֶם מִן הָאָרֶץ.	מוֹצִיא
מֶען לאָזט אָפ דִי אוּנטֶערשׁטֶע מַצָה אוּן מֶען מאַכט אַ בְּרָכָה עַל אֲכִילַת מַצָה. מֶען האַט אִין זִינֶען דִי בְּרָכָה זאָל פַטְרְ'ן אוֹיך דֶעם כּוֹרֵך אוּן דֶעם אַפִיקוֹמָן. מֶען עֶסט אַ כְּזַיִת פוּן יֶעדֶער פוּן דִי צְוֵוי מַצוֹת אָנגֶעלֶענטֶערהֵייט.	מַצָּה
מֶען טוּנקט אַיין אַ כְּזַיִת מָרוֹר אִין חֲרוֹסֶת. מֶען טרֵייסֶלט אָפ דִי חֲרוֹסֶת, אוּן מֶען מאַכט אַ בְּרָכָה עַל אֲכִילַת מָרוֹר. דִי מָרוֹר עֶסט מֶען נִיט אָנגֶעלֶענטֶערהֵייט.	מָרוֹר
מֶען טוּנקט אַיין אַ כְּזַיִת חֲזֶרֶת אִין חֲרוֹסֶת. מֶען טרֵייסֶלט אָפ דִי חֲרוֹסֶת. מֶען לֵייגְט דִי חֲזֶרֶת צְוִוישֶׁן צְוֵוי שׁטִיקֶעלאַך פוּן דִי אוּנטֶערשׁטֶע מַצָה. מֶען זאָגט כֵּן עָשָׂה הִלֵּל אוּן מֶען עֶסט דאָס אָנגֶעלֶענטֶערהֵייט.	כּוֹרֵך
מֶען גְרֵייט צוּם טִישׁ אוּן מֶען עֶסט סְעוּדַת יוֹם טוֹב.	שֻׁלְחָן עוֹרֵךְ
מֶען עֶסט אַ כְּזַיִת פוּן דֶעם אַפִיקוֹמָן אָנגֶעלֶענטֶערהֵייט. דֶערנאָך טאָר מֶען נִיט עֶסן (אוּן מֶען פִירט זִיך אוֹיך נִישׁט צוּ טרִינקֶן).	צָפוּן
מֶען גִיסט אָן דֶעם דְרִיטֶן כּוֹס, אוּן מֶען בֶּענטשׁט אוֹיף אִים בִּרְכַּת הַמָּזוֹן.	בָּרֵךְ
מֶען זאָגט הַלֵּל, פוּן לֹא לָנוּ בִּיזְן סוֹף.	הַלֵּל
אַז מֶען טוּט לוֹיט דֶעם דאָזִיגְן סֵדֶר אִיז מֶען בַּאוִויילִיגְט בַּיי דֶעם אוֹיבֶּערשׁטֶן, אוּן לְשָׁנָה הַבָּאָה בִּירוּשָׁלָיִם.	נִרְצָה

וּסְפַרְתֶּם לָכֶם מִמָּחֳרַת הַשַּׁבָּת...
שֶׁבַע שַׁבָּתוֹת תְּמִימֹת תִּהְיֶינָה (וַיִּקְרָא כג: טו)

AND YOU SHALL COUNT FOR YOURSELVES
FROM THE DAY AFTER THE HOLIDAY (PESACH)...
SEVEN COMPLETE WEEKS THEY SHALL BE.

EACH NIGHT, COUNT THE *SEFIRA* FOR THE NEXT DAY.

WEEK #	WED.	THURS	FRI.	שַׁבָּת קוֹדֶשׁ	SUN.	MON.	TUES.
❶	1	2	3	4	5	6	7
❷	8	9	10	11	12	13	14
❸	15	16	17	18	19	20	21
❹	22	23	24	25	26	27	28
❺	29	30	31	32	33	34	35
❻	36	37	38	39	40	41	42
❼	43	44	45	46	47	48	49
🌹	ת	ו	ע	ו	ב	שׁ	🌹

© Rabbi C.B. Alevsky 5767/2007

שְׁמִי _____ *SEFIRAT HA'OMER* CHART FOR YEAR 5768 / 2008 בס"ד

וּסְפַרְתֶּם לָכֶם מִמָּחֳרַת הַשַּׁבָּת...
שֶׁבַע שַׁבָּתוֹת תְּמִימֹת תִּהְיֶינָה (וַיִּקְרָא כג: טו)

AND YOU SHALL COUNT FOR YOURSELVES
FROM THE DAY AFTER THE HOLIDAY (PESACH)...
SEVEN COMPLETE WEEKS THEY SHALL BE.

EACH NIGHT, COUNT THE *SEFIRA* FOR THE NEXT DAY.

WEEK #	MON.	TUES.	WED.	THURS.	FRI.	שַׁבָּת קוֹדֶשׁ	SUN.
❶	1	2	3	4	5	6	7
❷	8	9	10	11	12	13	14
❸	15	16	17	18	19	20	21
❹	22	23	24	25	26	27	28
❺	29	30	31	32	33	34	35
❻	36	37	38	39	40	41	42
❼	43	44	45	46	47	48	49
🌹	ת	ו	ע	ו	ב	שׁ	🌹

© Rabbi C.B. Alevsky 5767/2007

שְׁמִי _____ *SEFIRAT HA'OMER* CHART FOR YEAR _____ בס"ד

AND YOU SHALL COUNT FOR YOURSELVES
FROM THE DAY AFTER THE HOLIDAY (PESACH)...
SEVEN COMPLETE WEEKS THEY SHALL BE.

וּסְפַרְתֶּם לָכֶם מִמׇּחֳרַת הַשַּׁבָּת...
שֶׁבַע שַׁבָּתוֹת תְּמִימֹת תִּהְיֶינָה (וַיִקְרָא כג: טו)

EACH NIGHT, COUNT THE *SEFIRA* FOR THE NEXT DAY.

WEEK #							
❶	1	2	3	4	5	6	7
❷	8	9	10	11	12	13	14
❸	15	16	17	18	19	20	21
❹	22	23	24	25	26	27	28
❺	29	30	31	32	33	34	35
❻	36	37	38	39	40	41	42
❼	43	44	45	46	47	48	49
🌹	ת	וֹ	ע	וּ	ב	שָׁ	🌹

© Rabbi C.B. Alevsky 5767/2007

שְׁמִי _____ *SEFIRAT HA'OMER* CHART FOR YEAR _____ בס"ד

AND YOU SHALL COUNT FOR YOURSELVES
FROM THE DAY AFTER THE HOLIDAY (PESACH)...
SEVEN COMPLETE WEEKS THEY SHALL BE.

וּסְפַרְתֶּם לָכֶם מִמׇּחֳרַת הַשַּׁבָּת...
שֶׁבַע שַׁבָּתוֹת תְּמִימֹת תִּהְיֶינָה (וַיִקְרָא כג: טו)

EACH NIGHT, COUNT THE *SEFIRA* FOR THE NEXT DAY.

WEEK #							
❶	1	2	3	4	5	6	7
❷	8	9	10	11	12	13	14
❸	15	16	17	18	19	20	21
❹	22	23	24	25	26	27	28
❺	29	30	31	32	33	34	35
❻	36	37	38	39	40	41	42
❼	43	44	45	46	47	48	49
🌹	ת	וֹ	ע	וּ	ב	שָׁ	🌹

© Rabbi C.B. Alevsky 5767/2007

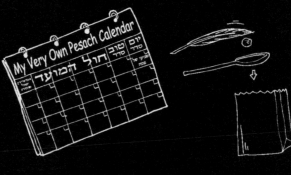

My Very Own

PESACH
Guide

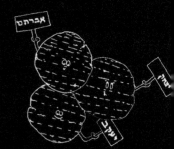

Review Questions

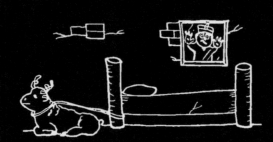

THE MONTH OF NISSAN - חוֹדֶשׁ נִיסָן

(See page 3 in Pesach Guide)

1. Write the Hebrew words from the Torah that tell us about Pesach, and their translation.

Translation	Words of Pasuk

2. What Holiday do we celebrate in נִיסָן, and what are we celebrating? (2)

_____

_____

3. Explain the two names given to the month of נִיסָן in the תּוֹרָה:

NAME	TRANSLATION	EXPLANATION
הַחֹדֶשׁ הָרִאשׁוֹן		
חוֹדֶשׁ הָאָבִיב		

4. What תְּפִילָה do we add to our daily routine during the month of נִיסָן? _____

WE SAY...	WHEN	WHY

5. Where in the חוּמָשׁ do we find this reading? _____

6. What kind of presents did the נְשִׂיאִים bring? _____

_____

_____

7. What is strange about the way they are listed in the Torah?_____

_____

_____

8. What lesson can we learn from this in our own lives? _____

_____

9. What *don't* we say during the month of נִיסָן? _____

מָעוֹת חִטִּים - MAOT CHITIM - MONEY FOR WHEAT (*MATZOT*)

(See page 6 in Pesach Guide)

1. Translate the following:

_____	כִּי יִהְיֶה בְךָ אֶבְיוֹן מֵאַחַד אַחֶיךָ....
_____	לֹא תְאַמֵּץ אֶת לְבָבְךָ וְלֹא תִקְפֹּץ אֶת יָדְךָ מֵאָחִיךָ הָאֶבְיוֹן
_____	כִּי פָתֹחַ תִּפְתַּח אֶת יָדְךָ לוֹ וְהַעֲבֵט תַּעֲבִיטֶנּוּ דֵּי מַחְסֹרוֹ אֲשֶׁר יֶחְסַר לוֹ (דברים טו:ז-ח)

10. write the name of this special צְדָקָה that is given during חוֹדֶשׁ נִיסָן. What is done with this money? _____

_____

11. Other than the usual Mitzvah of helping others out, what is another reasons for us to give this special צְדָקָה?_____

_____

_____

_____

12. In order to increase our appetite for the good tasting מַצָּה on פֶּסַח, we: _____

_____

13. Some people have the custom to do this from when? _____

_____

SHABBAT HAGGADOL – שַׁבָּת הַגָּדוֹל

(See page 7 in Pesach Guide)

14. The שַׁבָּת before פֶּסַח is called _____

15. What are few of the reasons for this name? (5)

a. _____

_____

b. _____

_____

c. _____

_____

d. _____

_____

e. _____

_____

16. Why do we celebrate שַׁבָּת הַגָּדוֹל specifically on שַׁבָּת? The נֵס happened on י' נִיסָן, and we usually celebrate a יוֹם טוֹב or any other special day, by its day of the month, not the day of the week? _____

_____

_____

17. On שַׁבָּת הַגָּדוֹל we say part of the _____:

WHEN	WHAT	WHY? (2)

חַג הַפֶּסַח – PESACH

(See page 10 in Pesach Guide)

18. . Translate the following Pesukim:

_____	אֶת חַג הַמַּצּוֹת תִּשְׁמֹר
_____	לְמוֹעֵד חֹדֶשׁ הָאָבִיב...
_____	...כִּי בוֹ יָצָאתָ מִמִּצְרַיִם (שמות כג: טו)
_____	...וְרָאִיתִי אֶת הַדָּם וּפָסַחְתִּי עֲלֵכֶם
_____	וְלֹא יִהְיֶה בָכֶם נֶגֶף לְמַשְׁחִית (שמות יב,יג)

19. . *Fill in the blanks:*

On פֶּסַח we celebrate that ה' took the _____ out of _____ on the ____ day of _____ in the year _____. The Jewish people were working as _____ for the _____, and ה' heard their cries. ה' hit מִצְרַיִם with 10 _____ and punished them for their cruelty to בְּנֵי יִשְׂרָאֵל.

ה' told בְּנֵי יִשְׂרָאֵל to offer a _____ for a קָרְבַּן פֶּסַח and smear some of its _____ onto the _____. Then, when he struck all the _____ of מִצְרַיִם He _____ the homes with the _____ on the doorposts. To remember this נֵס, the firstborn of each family _____.

We are instructed to celebrate פֶּסַח every year at this time, by eating _____, not eating _____ and by telling the story of _____.

* * * *

20. Draw a picture of how the Jews protected themselves during the final plague. What Hebrew letter does it resemble, and what was it hinting at?

THE מִצְווֹת OF חַג הַפֶּסַח

21. What Mitzvos do we learn from these Pesukim?

What	In the תּוֹרָה it says...
	כִּי כָּל אֹכֵל חָמֵץ וְנִכְרְתָה הַנֶּפֶשׁ הַהוּא מִיִשְׂרָאֵל מִיּוֹם הָרִאשֹׁן עַד יוֹם הַשְּׁבִיעִי (שמות יב:יז...)
	שִׁבְעַת יָמִים שְׂאֹר לֹא יִמָּצֵא בְּבָתֵּיכֶם
	...וְלֹא יֵרָאֶה לְךָ חָמֵץ...
	שִׁבְעַת יָמִים תֹּאכַל מַצּוֹת
	וְהִגַּדְתָּ לְבִנְךָ, בַּיּוֹם הַהוּא לֵאמֹר בַּעֲבוּר זֶה עָשָׂה ה' לִי בְּצֵאתִי מִמִּצְרָיִם (שמות יג:ח)

22. What is your favorite Mitzvah, and why?

_____

_____

_____

THE NAMES OF פֶּסַח

NAME	MEANING	EXPLANATION

23. So, what is it _really_ called...? 'ה - in the תּוֹרָה - calls this יוֹם טוֹב with one name, and we - בְּנֵי יִשְׂרָאֵל call it with a different name. We each have our own special reasons:

WHO	CALLS IT..	WHY
'ה		
בְּנֵי יִשְׂרָאֵל		

24. Rabbi לֵוִי יִצְחָק of _Berditchov_ explains the reason why there's a difference:

From בְּנֵי יִשְׂרָאֵל's point of view: _____

_____

From 'ה's point of view: _____

_____

The פֶּסַח calendar

25. The יוֹם טוֹב of פֶּסַח begins on (date)_____ and continues for ____(number of) days until (date) _____.

26. How many days of יוֹם טוֹב are we told to celebrate in the תּוֹרָה ? Which days are they? _____

_____

27. What did the חֲכָמִים add for those of us who live outside of אֶרֶץ יִשְׂרָאֵל?_____

28. What is this called? _____

29. If we lived in אֶרֶץ יִשְׂרָאֵל, we would keep which days of יוֹם טוֹב? _____

30. With which other יָמִים טוֹבִים does this occur? _____

_____

31. What are the days of פֶּסַח that are not יוֹם טוֹב called? _____

32. What are we allowed to do during this time, that is different than יוֹם טוֹב? _____

_____

33. What are the last two days of פֶּסַח called? _____

34. Fill in this calendar of Pesach based on the above information. Indicate what we do on those days (i.e. סֵדֶר) and what those days are called.

Date	Day	Day is called:	We...
טו נִיסָן	1		
טז נִיסָן	2		
יז נִיסָן	3		
חי נִיסָן	4		
יט נִיסָן	5		
כ נִיסָן	6		
כא נִיסָן	7		
כב נִיסָן	8		

35. In אֶרֶץ יִשְׂרָאֵל they celebrate only _____ day of יוֹם טוֹב in the beginning. They have only _____ סֵדֶר They celebrate _____ days of חוֹל הַמּוֹעֵד, and celebrate _____ and _____ on the same day, the ___ day.

CHAMETZ – חָמֵץ

(See page 16 in Pesach Guide)

36. Match the Pesukim to their translations:

You shall not eat any chometz...	שִׁבְעַת יָמִים מַצוֹת תֹּאכֵלוּ
And no Chometz may be seen in all your territories (boundaries) (Shmos: 13:7)	...בַּיוֹם הָרִאשׁוֹן תַּשְׁבִּיתוּ שְּׂאֹר מִבָּתֵּיכֶם (שְׁמוֹת יב:ט"ו)
During these seven days Chometz may not be found in your homes	שִׁבְעַת יָמִים שְׂאֹר לֹא יִמָּצֵא בְּבָתֵּיכֶם
No Chometz may be seen in your possession...	כִּי כָּל אֹכֵל חָמֵץ וְנִכְרְתָה הַנֶּפֶשׁ הַהוּא מִיִּשְׂרָאֵל... (שְׁמוֹת יב:יט...)
For seven days you should eat Matzos	כָּל מַחְמֶצֶת לֹא תֹאכֵלוּ...
For whoever will each Chometz, that soul will be cut off from (the community of) Israel	...וְלֹא יֵרָאֶה לְךָ חָמֵץ...
On the first day you should remove Chometz from your homes	וְלֹא-יֵרָאֶה לְךָ שְׂאֹר בְּכָל-גְּבֻלֶךָ (שְׁמוֹת יג:ז)

37. What is חָמֵץ?_____

_____

38. During פֶּסַח, even the minutest, tiniest amount of חָמֵץ is _____. What happens if a tiny amount of חָמֵץ falls into a large amount of "non-חָמֵץ?_____

_____

The Spiritual חָמֵץ

39. חָמֵץ is compared to what inside of you, and why? _____

_____

40. מַצָּה is compared to what inside of you, and why? _____

_____

41. What character trait is חָמֵץ like? how? _____

_____

42. What character trait is מַצָּה like? how? _____

_____

43. What can we learn from the מַצָּה? _____

_____

_____

44. What should we not learn from the חָמֵץ? _____

_____

_____

45. What do we learn from the words "חָמֵץ"and "מַצָּה"? How are they similar, and what makes them different? _____

_____

46. What can we learn from this? _____

_____

47. What other lesson in serving Hashem can we learn from חָמֵץ/מַצָּה? _____

_____

_____

48. What's the connection between a Bar Mitzvah and Bedikas Chometz? _____

_____

THE SEARCH FOR *CHOMETZ* – בְּדִיקַת חָמֵץ

(See page 19 in Pesach Guide)

49. The בְּדִיקָה is the beginning of which מִצְוָה? _____

50. When do we search for חָמֵץ? _____

_____

51. Where do we look? _____

52. What time of day do we conduct our search? _____

_____

53. How do we prepare our homes for the בְּדִיקָה? _____

_____

54. What do we hide around the house? why? _____

55. What kind of candle is the best to use for the בְּדִיקָה? What kind should not be used? ___

_____

_____

56. What do we use the feather and spoon for? _____

_____

57. What do we do with these items when we are done finding all the חָמֵץ? _____

_____

58. What בְּרָכָה does the head of the household we make before the search? Why? _____

_____

59. What should we not do during the בְּדִיקָה? _____

בס״ד

60. What do we say at the end of the בְּדִיקָה? _____

61. What language is it in, and why? _____

62. What should you do if you have more than one place to look for חָמֵץ? _____

63. What do you do... if you find חָמֵץ on פֶּסַח? _____

64. If you find it after פֶּסַח? _____

65. You are going away to a hotel for פֶּסַח, and plan to leave a week before פֶּסַח. What part of the בְּדִיקָה do you have to do at home? _____

66. When עֶרֶב פֶּסַח falls out on Shabbos, we do the בְּדִיקָה on _____.

Burning The Chometz – בִּיעוּר חָמֵץ

(See page 16 in Pesach Guide)

67. What's the difference between "לֹא יִמָּצֵא בְּבָתֵּיכֶם" and "וְלֹא יֵרָאֶה לְךָ חָמֵץ"? _____

_____

68. How can we get rid of the חָמֵץ, מִדְּאוֹרַיְיתָא? _____

69. What do our Rabbis tell us we must do? _____

_____

70. Even if we sell the חָמֵץ to a non Jew, we still need to hide it. Why? _____

_____

71. From what time on Erev Pesach are we forbidden to have חָמֵץ in our possession?

72. Why? _____

73. What time of day is it? _____

74. When do we do the בִּיעוּר חָמֵץ? _____

75. How do we do בִּיעוּר חָמֵץ? _____

_____

76. Why do we say כָּל חֲמִירָא again? _____

77. Why don't we say the שֶׁהֶחֱיָינוּ on the בִּיעוּר? _____

_____

SELLING THE CHOMETZ - מְכִירַת חָמֵץ

(See page 16 in Pesach Guide)

78. Why do we sell our חָמֵץ, and to whom? _____

_____

79. When can you NOT sell it? _____

_____

80. What do we do with the sold חָמֵץ? _____

81. What does the sale have to include? _____

82. If Shmerel sold his חָמֵץ, but in his heart he really thinks it belongs to him – what עֲבֵירָה did he commit? _____

_____

83. Who does the "selling of the חָמֵץ" for us? why? _____

_____

84. What is חָמֵץ שֶׁעָבַר עָלָיו הַפֶּסַח, and what is done with it? _____

WATCHED/GUARDED MATZAH – מַצָּה שְׁמוּרָה

85. The מַצָּה we use for פֶּסַח is called מַצָּה שְׁמוּרָה. What does this mean? _____

_____

86. If you only have a little bit of מַצָּה שְׁמוּרָה, when should you eat it on פֶּסַח? _____

87. When does the "careful watch" begin? _____

_____

88. What extra precautions do they take to make sure that there is no חָמֵץ in the מַצָּה
? _____

_____

89. What is מַיִם שֶׁלָּנוּ, and why do we use it for מַצָּה? _____

90. What do they do to the dough after it is rolled, and why? _____

_____

91. What words must the people working in the Matzah bakery say, and have in mind? _____

_____

_____

91. Why are some people careful not to get מַצָּה wet after it is baked? _____

_____

92. What are some of the other kinds of מַצָּה that can be eaten on פֶּסַח? _____

93. What are some kinds of מַצָּה that we do not use? _____

94. What are some of the reasons people say we should not use machine made מַצָּה? _____

_____

_____

_____

EREV PESACH   עֶרֶב פֶּסַח

(See page 30 in Pesach Guide)

95. When is עֶרֶב פֶּסַח?_____

96. What are some of the things we prepare on עֶרֶב פֶּסַח? _____

_____

97. What should we not eat on עֶרֶב פֶּסַח? _____

98. What do firstborns have to do on this day? why? _____

_____

99. What can they do to get out of it? _____

100 What do we say after מִנְחָה? why? _____

_____

101. What is קִטְנִיוֹת? _____

102. Who eats it on פֶּסַח, and who does not? _____

Pesach  **Questions**

THE קָרְבָּן WAY... *Match the translations to the pesukim.*

But only roasted by fire	...בֶּעָשֹׂר לַחֹדֶשׁ הַזֶּה וְיִקְחוּ לָהֶם אִישׁ שֶׂה לְבֵית אָבֹת שֶׂה לַבָּיִת... (שמות יב:ג)
Do not eat it raw or cooked in water	בְּבַיִת אֶחָד יֵאָכֵל לֹא-תוֹצִיא מִן הַבַּיִת מִן הַבָּשָׂר חוּצָה וְעֶצֶם לֹא תִשְׁבְּרוּ בוֹ (שמות יב:מו)
And you should not keep the sacrifice overnight – until the morning (Shmos 34:625	צְלִי אֵשׁ וּמַצּוֹת עַל מְרֹרִים יֹאכְלֻהוּ
Do not leave any of it for the next morning, and whatever remains until morning you shall burn in fire.	וְלֹא תוֹתִירוּ מִמֶּנּוּ עַד בֹּקֶר וְהַנֹּתָר מִמֶּנּוּ עַד בֹּקֶר בָּאֵשׁ תִּשְׂרֹפוּ
On the 10th of this month every man must take for himself a lamb for each family a lamb for each household *(Shmos 12:3)*	אַל תֹּאכְלוּ מִמֶּנּוּ נָא וּבָשֵׁל מְבֻשָּׁל בַּמָּיִם
Eat it roasted by fire – together with מָרוֹר and מַצּוֹת	כִּי אִם צְלִי אֵשׁ
And they should eat the meat on this night	וְלֹא יָלִין לַבֹּקֶר זֶבַח חַג הַפָּסַח (שמות לד:כה)
And the whole community of Israel shall Shecht it in the afternoon (Shmos 12:6)	וְהָיָה לָכֶם לְמִשְׁמֶרֶת עַד אַרְבָּעָה עָשָׂר יוֹם לַחֹדֶשׁ הַזֶּה
And you should hold it in safekeeping until the 14th day of this month	וְאָכְלוּ אֶת הַבָּשָׂר בַּלַּיְלָה הַזֶּה
It should be eaten in one house Do not take any of the meat out of the house and do not break any bones in it (Shmos 12:41)	וְשָׁחֲטוּ אֹתוֹ כֹּל קְהַל עֲדַת יִשְׂרָאֵל בֵּין הָעַרְבָּיִם (שמות יב:ו...)

104. In the times of the בֵּית הַמִּקְדָשׁ who offered the קָרְבָּן פֶּסַח? _____

105. Who would eat the meal? _____

106. Show how the Sefer Hachinuch explained how the laws of קָרְבַּן פֶּסַח symbolize royalty:

	The laws of the קָרְבָּן ...	THE ROYAL WAY...
❶		
❷		
❸		
❹		

ERUV TAVSHILIN – עֵירוּב תַּבְשִׁילִין

(See page 33 in Pesach Guide)

107. On יוֹם טוֹב and שַׁבָּת, we cannot prepare food for _____

108. What's the problem when יוֹם טוֹב comes out of Friday and Shabbos or Thursday and Friday? _____

_____

109. What is an עֵירוּב תַּבְשִׁילִין ? _____

_____

110. Who instituted it? _____

111. How do we make an עֵירוּב תַּבְשִׁילִין? _____

_____

112. Why do we make a עֵירוּב תַּבְשִׁילִין (2 reasons)? _____

_____

113. Who has to make one? _____

114. What's our "back up plan" if one family forgets? _____

115. What if they are just lazy, and don't bother? _____

116. What בְּרָכָה do we make on the עירוּב תַּבְשִׁילִין? _____

_____

הַדְלָקַת הַנֵּרוֹת – CANDLE LIGHTING

117. On יד נִיסָן in the evening before sunset, we light the יוֹם טוֹב candles. What בְּרָכוֹת do we say?

_____

118. Who is obligated to light? _____

119. What בְּרָכָה do we say if יוֹם טוֹב falls on שַׁבָּת? _____

120. Why do we light candles on יוֹם טוֹב? _____

121. What time should we light the first night? _____

122. When should we light the second night? _____

THE סֵדֶר PLATE

(See page 35 in Pesach Guide)

123. We prepare _____ (number) of מַצוֹת for the סֵדֶר.

124. Why that amount? (3 reasons) a. _____

_____

b. _____

_____

c. _____

_____

125. The סֵדֶר plate itself, called the_____ has six things on it.

126. Draw the six items, and write their names, in the spaces below:

THE סֵדֶר PLATE, CONTINUED

127. What *do we use for the* זְרוֹעַ ? _____

128. What does it symbolize? _____

129. Why is it called זְרוֹעַ? what does it refer to? _____

_____

130. Why *do we use chicken and not meat?* _____

131. How else *do we remind ourselves of this during the* סֵדֶר? _____

132. What does the בֵּיצָה represent? _____

_____

133. What's the "eggs-tremely" important message of the egg? a. _____

_____

b. _____

_____

134. What *do we use for* מָרוֹר ? _____

135. Why *do we eat it?* _____

136. What is חֲרוֹסֶת? What's it made from? _____

137. When *do we eat it?* _____

138. What does the texture of this mixture remind us of? _____

139. What do all the separate ingredients remind us of? (4) _____

_____

_____

140. What *do we use for* כַּרְפַּס ? _____

141. What *do we dip it in? why?* _____

142. When you mix up the letters of כַּרְפַּס, what words do we get? _____

143. What do they mean? _____

_____

144. What do we use for חֲזֶרֶת? _____

145. When do we eat the חֲזֶרֶת? _____

146. Why do we use this vegetable? _____

THE FOUR CUPS – ד' כּוֹסוֹת

(See page 39 in Pesach Guide)

147. During the סֵדֶר we drink _____ cups of wine. Why do we need each one?

1. _____

2. _____

3. _____

4. _____

148. What does the *Maharal* say the four cups are compared to? _____

149. What does the *Abarbanel* say the four cups are compared to? _____

_____

_____

_____

Pesach

Questions

150. What are the four expressions of the redemption that the four cups are connected to?

1. _____

2. _____

3. _____

4. _____

151. What's the fifth expression, and what cup goes with that expression? _____

_____

152. Why don't we make a בְּרָכָה on the מִצְוָה of drinking the four cups of wine? (2 reasons) _____

_____

_____

_____

153. What Mitzvos does the red in our wine symbolize? _____

_____

_____

_____

THE סֵדֶר – סֵדֶר – ORDER OF THE NIGHT

(See page 42 in Pesach Guide)

154. What does סֵדֶר mean, literally? _____

155. Why did the חֲכָמִים call our Pesach meal a סֵדֶר ? _____

וְהִגַּדְתָּ לְבִנְךָ: What doe we have to tell our children? _____

157. How do the חֲכָמִים prevent the children from falling asleep during the סֵדֶר ? _____

_____

158. We sometimes act like kings during the סֵדֶר, and sometimes like poor people. List two examples of each "style" of dining: _____

_____

_____

159. Why do we express both of these feelings? _____

_____

160. What is the deeper message here? _____

_____

_____

161. Number the סֵדֶר (סִימָנֵי הַסֵּדֶר Signs) in the correct order.

מַגִּיד	מָרוֹר	הַלֵּל	נִרְצָה
שֻׁלְחָן עוֹרֵךְ	יַחַץ	מוֹצִיא	רָחְצָה
קַדֵּשׁ	מַצָּה	כַּרְפַּס	וּרְחַץ
צָפוּן	בָּרֵךְ	כּוֹרֵךְ	

סִימָנֵי הַסֵּדֶר – THE SEDER SIGNS

162. Why do we make קִידוּשׁ at the סֵדֶר? _____

163. How is the קִידוּשׁ different from a regular שַׁבָּת or יוֹם טוֹב? (2) _____

_____

164. What do some do before קִידוּשׁ that reminds us that we are "royal" at the סֵדֶר_____

_____

165. How are we supposed to drink our wine? _____

_____

166. Why do we wash our hands at וּרְחַץ? _____

_____

167. How is it different than washing for bread? _____

168. If we don't do this all year 'round, why are we careful the night of the סֵדֶר? _____

_____

169. What are some of the vegetables used for כַּרְפַּס? _____

170. In what position do sit when we eat the כַּרְפַּס? Why? _____

_____

171. How much of the vegetable should we eat? Why? _____

172. Why do we dip the vegetable in the salt water? _____

_____

173. Why do we break the מַצָּה? _____

174. What do we break at יַחַץ? Why that מַצָּה? _____

_____

175. Which piece do we set aside for the אֲפִיקוֹמָן? Why that one? _____

_____

176. Why is this מַצָּה called לֶחֶם עוֹנִי? _____

_____

177. What's another interpretation of the word עוֹנִי? _____

_____

178. What do we do during מַגִּיד? _____

179. With which words does מַגִּיד begin? _____
End? _____

180. What expression is the word הַגָּדָה derived from? _____

_____

181. Why don't we make a בְּרָכָה before reading the הַגָּדָה, if it's a מִצְוָה? (at least two
reasons) _____

_____

_____

_____

182. What should we have visible in front of us when we say הָא לַחְמָא עַנְיָא? _____

_____

183. What's the only מִצְוָה at the סֵדֶר that's מִדְאוֹרַיְיתָא? _____

184. Why not the other items on the סֵדֶר plate? _____

185. In הָא לַחְמָא עַנְיָא, who are we inviting? _____ What's funny about
this invitation? _____

_____

186. How is this invitation really a cry to Hashem to bring Moshiach? _____

_____

_____

187. What does יֵיתֵי וְיִפְסַח mean? _____

188. What does it refer to now? _____

189. Why do we learn from the fact that we say "this year we are here" twice? _____

_____

THE מַה נִּשְׁתַּנָּה – FOUR QUESTIONS

(See page 51 in Pesach Guide)

190. What do we do right before the מַה נִּשְׁתַּנָּה ? _____

191. From which Pasuk do we learn that our children are supposed to ask the מַה נִּשְׁתַּנָּה? _____

192. What does the fact that Tisha B'Av and Pesach always fall out on the same day of the year teach us? _____

_____

_____

193. Who should ask the Four Questions? _____

194. Why do we ask specifically *these* Four Questions? _____

_____

195. How does the Abarbanel explain the choice of these Four Questions? _____

_____

196. Why don't we ask about the Four Cups of wine? (at least two reasons) _____

_____

_____

_____

197. What is the answer to the Four Questions? _____

198. How does it answer these questions? _____

199. What does it mean, "If Hashem had not brought us out, we would still be slaves?" What if we left on our own? _____

_____

200. Why does Torah list all the Four sons individually, and together as a family? _____

_____

201. What does the חָכָם ask? _____

202. What does his question show? _____

203. How do we answer him? _____

204. Why do we tell him to not to eat the אֲפִיקוֹמָן? _____

_____

205. Why does the חָכָם say "you" if he is not excluding himself from the laws, like the רָשָׁע? (At least two reasons) _____

_____

_____

206. Why is the חָכָם near the רָשָׁע? _____

207. What does the רָשָׁע ask? _____

208. How do we answer him? _____

209. Why should we "blunt his teeth"? _____

210. What does the תם ask? _____

211. How do we answer him? _____

212. Who is the שאינו יודע לשאול? _____

213. What do we do to teach him? _____

214. What does the portion beginning with מִתְּחִילָה... talk about? _____

_____

215. וְהִיא שֶׁעָמְדָה : What stood by us? When? _____

_____

216. What's the גְּמַטְרִיָא of וְהִיא hint to? _____

_____

217. What were the ten מַכּוֹת? _____

_____

218. What are the two customs people do when we list these מַכּוֹת during the סֶדֶר? _____

_____

219. What do both of these customs teach us? _____

_____

_____

220. דְּצַ"ךְ עַדַ"שׁ בְּאַחַ"ב – What do these words mean? _____

_____

221. What is the "theme, idea" of דַּיֵּינוּ? _____

222. What does רַבָּן גַּמְלִיאֵל say we need to do to fulfill our obligation for the סֶדֶר? _____

_____

223. Why do we wash our hands the second time, during רָחְצָה? _____

_____

224. What is the first בְּרָכָה we recite over the מַצָּה ? _____

225. How do we hold the מַצָּה during the בְּרָכָה? _____

226. What is the second בְּרָכָה we recite? What should we have in mind at that time?_____

_____

_____

227. How much מַצָּה do we have to eat? _____

228. In which position should we sit to eat our מַצָּה? _____

229. How much מָרוֹר do we eat? _____

230. What do we dip it in? _____

231. What בְּרָכָה do we say? _____

232. In which position should we sit to eat our מָרוֹר? _____

233. What's כּוֹרֵךְ? Who instituted it? _____

_____

234. What do we say before eating it? _____

235. What's שֻׁלְחָן עוֹרֵךְ? _____

236. What do we eat for "dessert"? _____

237. What can't we do after the אֲפִיקוֹמָן? _____

238. When do we have to eat the אֲפִיקוֹמָן? _____

239. Why do some people hide the אֲפִיקוֹמָן? _____

_____

240. What do we add in the בִּרְכַּת הַמָזוֹן for Pesach?_____

241. What do we do immediately after the בִּרְכַּת הַמָזוֹן? _____

242. Who comes to visit us all on פֶּסַח night? Why?_____

_____

243. What do we put out for him? _____

244. Why do we walk to the door with candles when we say ... שְׁפֹךְ? _____

_____

245. What do we say in הַלֵּל? _____

246. When do we drink the last cup? _____

247. What is נִרְצָה mean?_____

248. With what special prayer do we end the whole סֵדֶר? _____

_____

A Bit About the תְּפִילוֹת

(See page 60 in Pesach Guide)

249. What do we add in בִּרְכַּת הַמָזוֹן and שְׁמוֹנֶה עֶשְׂרֵה? _____

250. What else do we add in our Davening?_____

251. What special שְׁמוֹנֶה עֶשְׂרֵה do we say on first two and last two days? ____

252. What are the first nights of פֶּסַח called ? Why?_____

_____

253. What do we not say during this time? _____

254. What do some other people do during this time?_____

255. On the first day, we STOP saying _____ during תְּפִילַת_____ .

256. Some people have a custom to say _____ on שַׁבָּת-חוֹל הַמוֹעֵד.

Chol Hamoed - חוֹל הַמוֹעֵד

(See page 72 in Pesach Guide)

257. During חוֹל הַמוֹעֵד, when are we are permitted to "work" or do מְלָאכוֹת? _____

_____

258. Why are we allowed to drive? _____

259. What can't we do on חוֹל הַמוֹעֵד? _____

260. When are you allowed to write? _____

261. When are you allowed to wash clothes? _____

The Seventh Day of Pesach – שְׁבִיעִי שֶׁל פֶּסַח

(See page 73 in Pesach Guide)

262. Translate these words:

	וּבַיוֹם הָרִאשׁוֹן מִקְרָא קֹדֶשׁ וּבַיוֹם הַשְּׁבִיעִי מִקְרָא קֹדֶשׁ יִהְיֶה לָכֶם
	כָּל מְלָאכָה לֹא יֵעָשֶׂה בָהֶם
	אַךְ אֲשֶׁר יֵאָכֵל לְכָל נֶפֶשׁ הוּא לְבַדּוֹ יֵעָשֶׂה לָכֶם... (שְׁמוֹת יב,טז)

263. Do we say שֶׁהֶחֱיָינוּ on the last days of פֶּסַח? Why? _____

_____

264. What great miracle do we remember on this day? _____

265. Why do we stay awake the night before שְׁבִיעִי שֶׁל פֶּסַח? _____

_____

266. What do some communities do that night? _____

_____

267. Why doesn't the Torah mention the date קְרִיעַת יַם סוּף happened? _____

The Last Day of Pesach – אַחֲרוֹן שֶׁל פֶּסַח

(See page 74 in Pesach Guide)

268. What תְּפִילָה is said on the last day? _____

269. What are some people lenient about on the last day? Why? _____

_____

_____

270. What special meal did the Baal Shem Tov introduce that many Chassidim do the last day of Pesach? _____

271. What is your favorite part of Pesach? _____

272. Why do we have to wait an hour after Pesach before we can eat our חָמֵץ? _____

_____

273. What do we start to count on the second night of פֶּסַח? _____

274. What kind of קָרְבָּן was brought on the second day of פֶּסַח? _____

_____

275. How many weeks do we count? _____

276. What's the 50th day? _____

277. What בְּרָכָה do we make on this מִצְוָה? _____

278. What happens if you forget to count one day? _____

_____

279. What happens if you forget for more than two days in a row? _____

_____

280. Are women obligated to do this מִצְוָה? Why do they still say the בְּרָכָה? _____

_____

CPSIA information can be obtained
at www.ICGtesting.com
Printed in the USA
LVHW061955250322
714400LV00016B/1269